Bon Appétit!

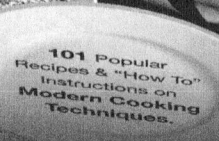

101 Popular Recipes & "How To" Instructions on **Modern Cooking Techniques**.

MODERN COOKING TECHNIQUES

YOU SUCK AT Sous Vide! THE COOKBOOK

101 CAN'T-MISS RECIPES WITH ILLUSTRATED INSTRUCTIONS FOR THE INEPT, THE COWARDLY, AND THE HOPELESS IN THE KITCHEN.

BOOKS BY YET ANOTHER
CELEBRITY CHEF

HHF

HEALTHY HAPPY FOODIE PRESS
SAN FRANCISCO, CA

COPYRIGHT © 2019 Healthy Happy Foodie Press (HHF Press)

First published 2019

All rights reserved. No part of this book may be reproduced in any form or by any electronic or mechanical means, including information storage and retrieval systems, without permission in writing from the publisher, except by reviewers, who may quote brief passages in a review.

Editor: HHF Press

Art Direction: HHF Press

Illustrations: HHF Press

All photographs in this book © HHF Press or © Depositphotos.com

Published in the United States of America by HHF Press
268 Bush St, #3042
San Francisco, CA 94104 USA
www.HHFPress.com

ISBN: 978-1-949314-06-9

Disclaimer:

Although the publisher and author of this book are practically obsessed with modern cooking techniques, neither represent, nor are associated or affiliated with, any of the brands mentioned in this text.

All content herein represents the author's own experiences and opinions, and do not represent medical or health advice. The responsibility for the consequences of your actions, including your use or misuse of any suggestion or procedure described in this book lies not with the authors, publisher or distributors of this book. We recommend consulting with a licensed health professional before changing your diet or exercise. The author or the publisher does not assume any liability for the use of or inability to use any or all of the information contained in this book, nor does the author or publisher accept responsibility for any type of loss or damage that may be experienced by the user as the result of activities occurring from the use of any information in this book. Use the information responsibly and at your own risk.

The author reserves the right to make changes he or she deems required to future versions of the publication to maintain accuracy.

Want to... JOIN THE HHF BOOK REVIEW CLUB?

Get the book "Modern Cooking Techniques," featuring 100 recipes and instructions for 10 surprising, time-saving modern kitchen tools such as spiralizers, air fryers, sous vide, instant-pots, dehydrators and more. FREE when you join!

Join today! *(It's completely FREE)*

Members get:
- A FREE copy of "Modern Cooking Techniques"
- 1 FREE cookbook every month (we will ask for your feedback)
- Participate in our "advance copy" community so you can influence our upcoming books!

Join today at:

www.JoinTheBookReviewClub.com/19-a2

Reader Reviews

Yes, I'm an idiot in the kitchen. My wife bought me this book and at first I laughed, but then I read it and tried some recipes. It's actually a really well thought-out book that taught me how to make amazing sous vide steaks and other incredible dishes. This is my favorite book at the moment.

David B.

I loved this book! It looks great, the pictures are beautiful, and the text is easy to read. I love the font size and overall feel of the book, it's really nicely produced. I loved the 10 minute start section that held my hand through making my first sous vide steak, which turned out delicious!!!

Sonia C.

Thanks for the clear and unfluffy text. I'm so tired of cookbooks that are full of useless information and anecdotes. You've done a great job of providing all of the useful info I needed to understand sous vide and be successful with it. I made my first steak a few days ago, and since then I've made sous vide fish, chicken, and oso buco. I'm hooked...

Tom M.

Great recipes in this book! I've already tried the shrimp, steak, and even a cake recipe. They were all fabulous beyond my expectations. This book looks good, tastes good, and I'm very happy to have it in my kitchen!

Wanda W.

Have you ever had sous vide filet mignon? That has become my family's favorite meal because it's better than anything we've ever had at a restaurant! This cooking method is magical...it almost easily beats any restaurant I've ever been to. And it has become my secret weapon when cooking for friends. You can't imagine how satisfying it is to be complimented over and over again by friends for "that amazing steak you made for us"...

Kathy P.

Why You Need This Book:

Immediately Stop Sucking at Sous Vide!

Illustrated instructions, a quick start guide and beyond-the-manual tips and tricks will teach you how to stop making mistakes and master your sous vide so that it becomes your favorite way to cook just about anything.

Learn Fast With Our "10 Minute Quick-Start"

Our illustrated "10 Minute Quick-Start" chapter will allow even the most inept chef to make a complete meal in under 10 minutes, so you can quickly enjoy delicious meats, vegetables, breakfast, desserts, and much more instead of spending all of your time apologizing to your guests and wondering what went wrong.

Clear, Illustrated Instructions

Look, we know sous vide sounds weird, and scary, and French, but this guide will make your sous vide experience so simple you can start cooking in minutes while avoiding stupid mistakes such as wrong settings, wrong timing, etc. Stop wasting your whole day watching videos on the internet and start cooking!

Go Beyond the Instruction Manual

Once you've become halfway decent at cooking sous vide, we're going to teach you the Pro tips that will have you cooking like restaurant chefs in no time. Learn the science behind sous vide cooking so that you can confidently make meals that won't make your friends and family gag.

All the Recipes You'll Ever Need!

101 of the best recipes on the planet will allow you to stop serving the same old boring meals night after night. Your family is sick of eating dry chicken and overcooked steak. Our recipes will let you branch out and help you stop sucking at sous vide.

Contents

ABOUT COOKING Sous Vide 1

HOW TO COOK Sous Vide 7

10 Minute Quick-Start 12-13

Pro Tips 15

Breakfast Dishes 19
    Hearty Sous Vide Pumpkin Bread............................ 20
    Perfect Eggs with Avocado Toast 21
    Cinnamon French Toast.. 22
    Asparagus & Feta Flan 24
    Sous Vide Overnight Oatmeal................................ 25
    Soft Poached Eggs In Hashbrown Nests 26
    Egg Yolk Croquette.. 27

Main Dishes: Beef & Lamb 29
    Juicy French Dip Sandwiches................................ 30
    Awesome Burgers 31
    Tenderest Steak & Buttery Potatoes 32
    Savory Pastrami 33
    Succulent Spaghetti and Meatballs 34
    Sous Vide Flat Iron Steak...................................... 36
    Sunday Eye Of Round Roast.................................. 37
    Mouth-Watering Steak Sashimi with Ponzu Dressing.......... 38
    Juicy Beef Brisket.. 39
    Slow-Cooked Pot Roast 41
    Fragrant Beef Bourguignon................................... 42

    Sweet-Savory Miso-Glazed Beef Steaks................. 43
    Satisfying Spicy Corned Beef................................ 44
    Melt-In-Your-Mouth Grilled Flank Steak.................. 45
    Decadent Lamb Steak with Red Wine Sauce............ 46
    Lamb Chops with Basil Chimichurri........................ 47

Main Dishes: Poultry 49
    Easy Chicken Cordon Bleu 50
    Succulent Sous Vide Duck Breasts......................... 51
    Aromatic Lemon Thyme Chicken............................ 52
    Rich and Tasty Duck à l'Orange.............................. 53
    The Moist Delicious Thanksgiving Turkey 55
    Spicy Honey Sriracha Wings 56
    Delicate Rosemary Chicken................................... 57
    Flavorful Chicken Marsala.................................... 58
    Tempting Teriyaki Chicken 59
    Tender Turkey Breast 60
    Sous Vide Chicken Breast with Creamy Mushroom Sauce..... 61

Main Dishes: Pork 63
    Melt-In-Your Mouth Carnitas for Tacos.................... 64
    Sous Vide Beer Brined Pork Shoulder 65
    Pork Tenderloin with Cherry Salsa.......................... 66

- Lemongrass and Garlic Roast Pork Belly Roll 67
- Juicy and Tender Pork Belly 68
- Simply Delicious Pork Chops 69
- Lemony Herb Crusted Pork Chops 71
- Yummy Pulled Pork with Chili Pepper BBQ Sauce 72
- Mouth-Water Bacon-Wrapped Pork Tenderloin 73
- Beer-Infused Sausages 74
- Oh-So-Tender Baby Back Ribs 75
- Kung Pao Short Ribs 76
- Scrumptious BBQ Ribs 77

Main Dishes: Seafood 79

- Sous Vide Cajun Tilapia 80
- Low-Tech High-Taste Salmon with Herb Butter 81
- Delightful Crispy Skin Salmon 82
- Coconut Party Shrimp 83
- Richly Intense Brown Butter Scallops 85
- Paccheri Pasta with Clams 86
- Delicious Dungeness Crab 87
- Easy Lobster Tails 88
- Luxurious Butter-Poached Lobster 89
- Oysters Sous Vide 90
- Light and Lemony Octopus 92
- Mediterranean-Style Tilapia with Tomato, Olives & Oregano ... 93
- Lovely Lobster Pasta 94
- Maple Bourbon Pecan Salmon 95

Vegetables & Side Dishes 97

- Sweet Potato Infused with Smoked Garlic, Paprika & Maple Syrup ... 98
- Butternut Squash & Apple Soup 99
- Sous Vide Honey-Glazed Carrots 100
- Rich Cream Corn with Crispy Parmesan 101
- Sous Vide Artichokes 103
- Doenjang-Spiced Eggplant 104

- Garlicky Brussels Sprouts 105
- Creamy Mashed Potatoes with Garlic and Rosemary 106
- Tasty Garlic Chili Tofu 107
- Naturally Delicious Asparagus 108
- Yummy Steak Fries 110
- Uni Chawanmushi 111
- Garlic Cheese Risotto 112
- Fluffy Sushi Rice 113
- Delicate and Tasty Mushrooms 114
- Rich and Hearty Polenta 115

Sauces & Condiments 117

- Creamy Hollandaise Sauce 118
- Sous Vide Flavor-Packed Pickles 119
- Easy Rich Tomato Sauce 121
- Tangy Southwest Pickled Onions 122
- Hot Chili Chutney 123
- Holiday Cranberry Sauce 124
- Creamy Béarnaise Sauce 126
- Classic Pickled Onions 127
- Spicy Pickled Pineapple 128
- Pickled Husk Cherries 129

Desserts 131

- Easy Sous Vide Dulce De Leche 132
- Yummy Flourless Chocolate Cake 133
- Decadent Leche Flan 134
- Vanilla Creme Brûlée 135
- Gooey Chocolate Chip Cookies 136
- Mason Jar Salted Caramel Cheesecake 137
- Delicate Honey Lavenderw Poached Peaches 138
- Apple Cranberry Pie 140
- Mini Lemon Cheesecakes 141
- Bourbon Infusion Apple Pie 142
- Sweet Meyer Lemon Cheesecake with Raspberry Sauce .. 143
- Sous Vide Lemon Curd 144
- Elegant Red Wine Poached Pears 145

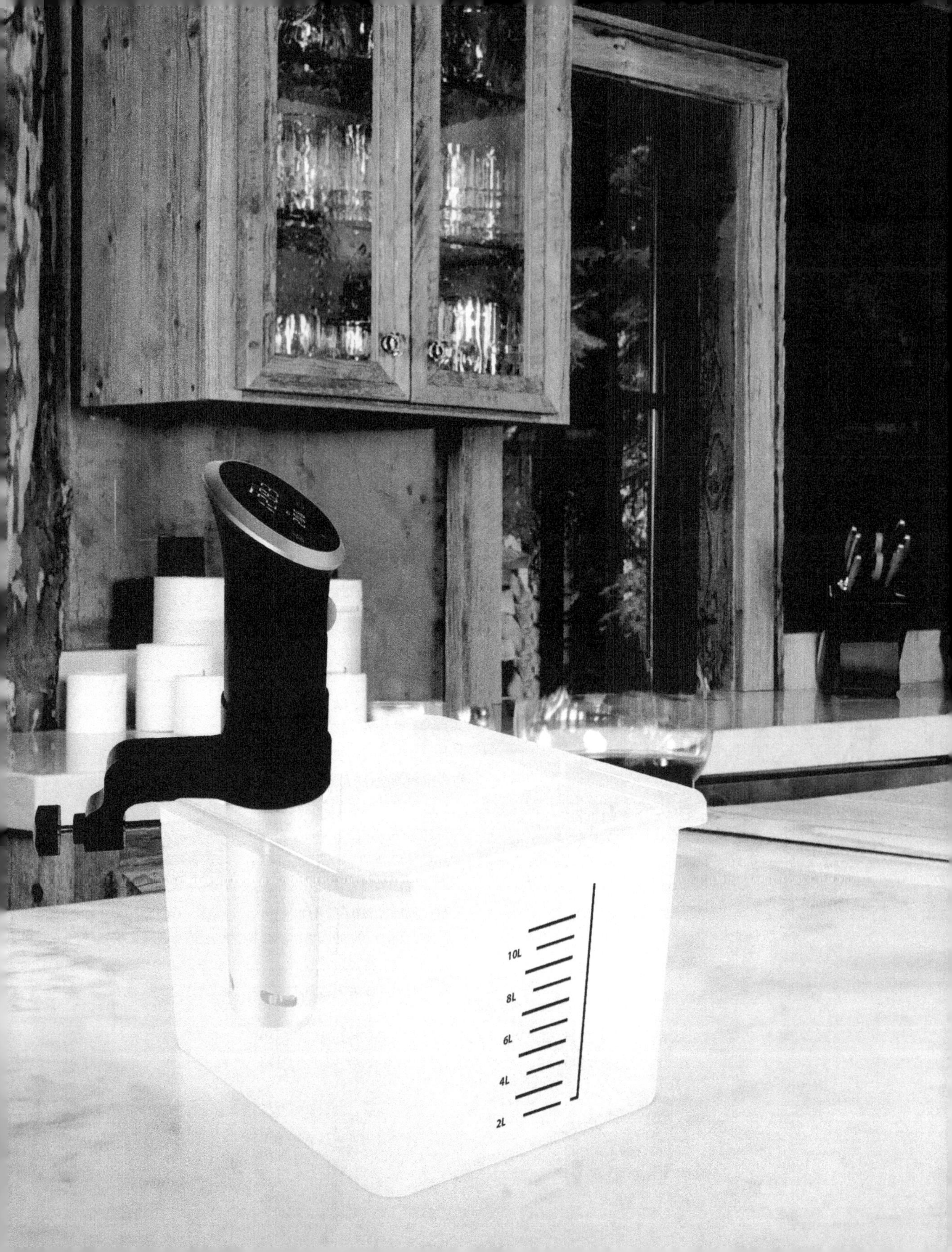
10L
8L
6L
4L
2L

CHAPTER 1

About Cooking
Sous Vide

What Is Sous Vide, and What Does It Do?

It might sound weird but, sous vide cooking is a method in which food is sealed in a bag, submerged in a water bath, and gradually brought to a specific temperature. Why is temperature important? Well, if you're asking this, you really need help... While there are many advantages to sous vide cooking, the most obvious is that it will be virtually impossible to overcook your food. All you need are a sous vide circulator, a container (bucket), and some large zipperlock bags. As you might have guessed the circulator circulates the water to make sure it is always set to the exact temperature that you want. Because of this, the food in the water bath will never rise above or fall below that temperature, so you never run the risk of over or undercooking anything. Sous vide is, quite literally, idiot proof.

"So, I just put my food in a zipperlock bag and drop it in the water bath?"

No, that won't work at all. Let's talk about the vide part for a second. In French, vide means vacuum, and if your food isn't vacuum sealed, it won't cook evenly. Simple food sealing devices like the FoodSaver make the process fast, easy, and reliable. But if you don't feel like dropping a bunch of cash on yet another piece of equipment, you can achieve a good seal using the water displacement method. Simply place your food in a zipper lock bag and seal all but a small corner of the zipper lock. Then, slowly submerge the bag in the water bath (make sure the water isn't too hot when you do this or you will burn your hand and look foolish). As you submerge the bag, the air will be forced out through the unsealed corner of the bag. When only this corner is above the surface of the water, pinch the zipper lock shut and all of the air will be removed.

What Does Sous Vide Not Do?

You can't fry chicken in a sous vide. Don't even try it. Cooking sous vide is all about internal temperature, but there are other aspects of cooking like searing, frying, and baking which require additional processes. While sous vide cooking is a great way to prepare food for searing or frying, you will still need additional equipment to accomplish these finishing steps.

Who Is It Good For?

Do you like making perfectly cooked dishes but have no real understanding of cooking? Are you constantly frustrated by overcooked or undercooked meals? Because it is so easy and fool proof, even the culinarily challenged can benefit from sous vide cooking because it makes it nearly impossible for you to screw it up. Once you have become familiar with the basic preparation process, you will find that cooking sous vide is a great way to finally make it look like you know what you are doing in the kitchen.

Sous vide cooking was originally used by high-end professional kitchens by chefs, who were already amazing at cooking, to improve efficiency when high volumes of food needed to be prepared quickly. But recently home cooks started realized sous vide is the absolute best way to make sure you don't ruin dinner. For beginner chefs it is the perfect way to ensure that you never over or undercook food. Busy professionals who also love ribs will appreciate the fact that you can sous vide a rack while at work all day and come home to perfectly fall off the bone texture and rich, balanced flavor.

Who Is It Not Good For?

If your cooking routine is: remove package from freezer, poke a few holes in the film, microwave, and serve, sous vide cooking may not be for you. Sous vide cooking often takes time, but not much effort, so if you're not willing to have a little patience, then sous vide cooking is not the method for you.

A Few Cautions

This might seem obvious, but water and electricity don't get along very well. Because we don't want you to electrocute yourself, always make sure the plug on your sous vide circulator has not come into contact with water while it is plugged in. Always make sure the plug is dry before inserting into an outlet, and try to keep your water bath as far as possible from electrical outlets.

To make sure your sous vide circulator remains in proper working order, you will need to take proper care of it. Since it will be submerged in a water bath for long periods of time while cooking, always make sure to remove it from the water as soon as cooking has finished and dry it thoroughly to prevent corrosion.

Your sous vide circulator has moving parts which are necessary to keep the water circulating in the container. While cooking, it is important to make sure nothing enters the slots in the circulator. Don't put your fingers in the slots! Foreign objects (like food or fingers) can damage the circulator, so make sure that your food items (and fingers) are securely away from the circulator.

What Are the Health Benefits of Sous Vide Cooking?

Everyone is concerned about getting proper nutrition, right? But what you may not know is that certain cooking methods can pointlessly destroy some of the vital nutrients that our bodies need. As they become delicious, many types of food, including meats and vegetables, can lose a great deal of their nutrients while being cooked over high heat. Some fat based nutrients can simply break down and become less beneficial, while others are lost as the juices cook out of the food. But this doesn't have to happen! With sous vide cooking you keep those awesome nutrients because sous vide uses much lower temperatures. As a result, the nutrients survive and help you survive as long as possible. And since the juices are all contained within the vacuum-sealed bag, they don't have anywhere to go. And that means... we're going to make gravy.

A Brief History of Sous Vide Cooking

The term sous vide is French for "under vacuum," which describes the main feature of sous vide cooking. In order to successfully cook sous vide it is necessary to submerge the food in a water bath in a vacuum-sealed bag. Sous vide is a cooking method that originated in France as early as 1799 as a method for reliable cooking and food preservation. Without special equipment, however, maintaining a constant temperature was laughably difficult and required constant supervision. Cooks of this era also didn't have the luxury of modern plastic bags and relied instead on animal intestines and bladders, which was gross and didn't maintain a perfect air tight seal. While the method provided impressive results, it was not a technique that most people had any interest in.

Modern Sous Vide Equipment

It wasn't until the 1970s, when sous vide immersion circulators became available, that French chefs discovered that sous vide was the perfect way to cook fois gras. Note: fois gras is delicious and also illegal in some states. They found that using this method, they were able to cook the cruel yet delicate goose liver pâté and maintain its original appearance; it also helped to retain the rich fat while cooking thoroughly. It wasn't long before other chefs began seeing the benefits of sous vide cooking. Now it is a widely used method for cooking many different types of foods and is found in professional kitchens around the world. These days, home sous vide units are state-of-the-art pieces of technology, with many employing Bluetooth capability, smartphone apps, and very few animal intestines.

Better Than Conventional Cooking?

The secret of sous vide cooking is control. All foods have an ideal internal temperature which determines how "done" it will end up being. This, combined with the amount of time the food is held at that temperature, will affect the food's texture. For things like steaks, conventional cooking says you use very high heat for a short period of time to produce a perfect result. Sous vide cooking takes a little longer but because it holds the food at precisely the right temperature, you will end up with perfect texture and reliable results. In short, sous vide is way better than poking a steak with your thumb to see if it's done.

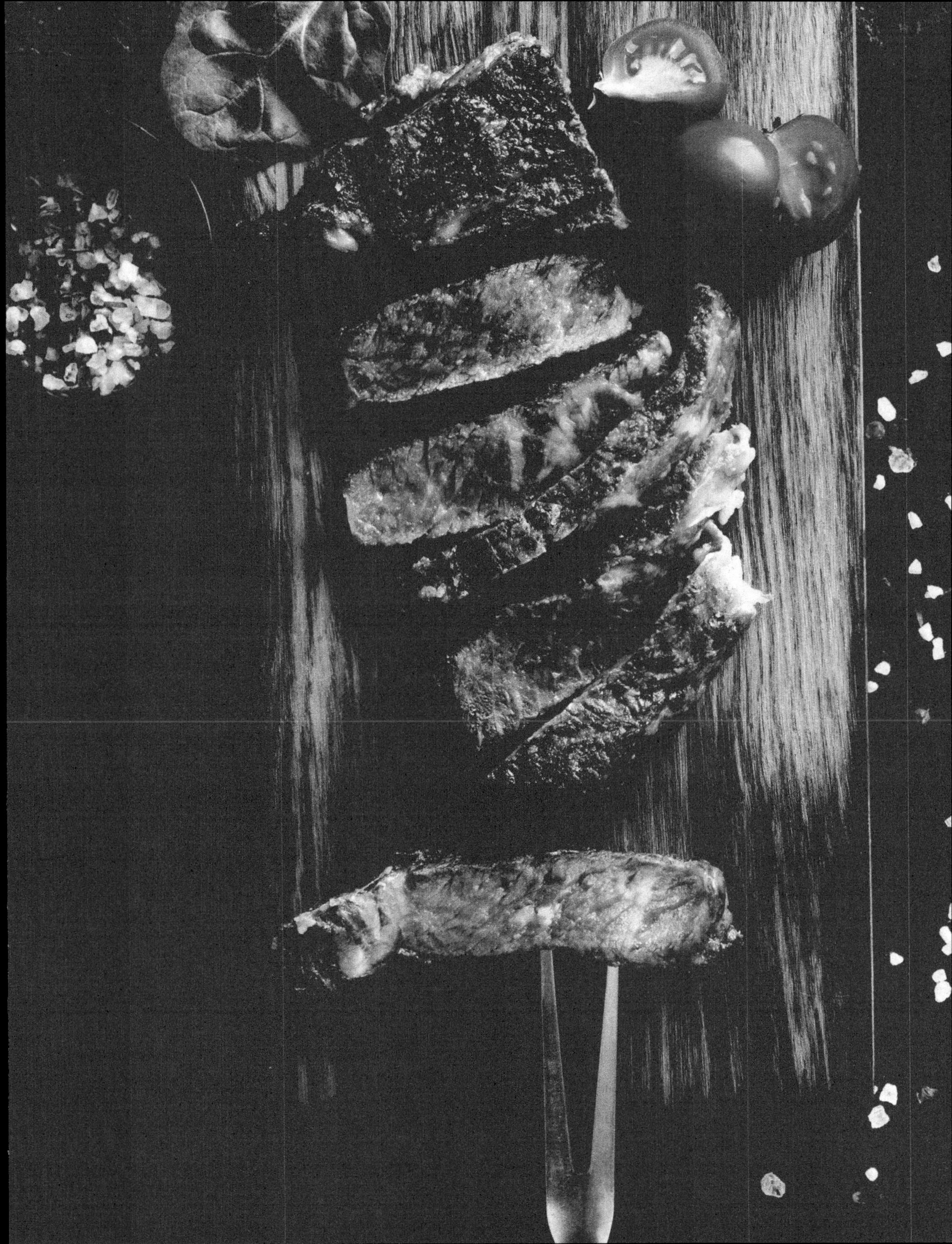

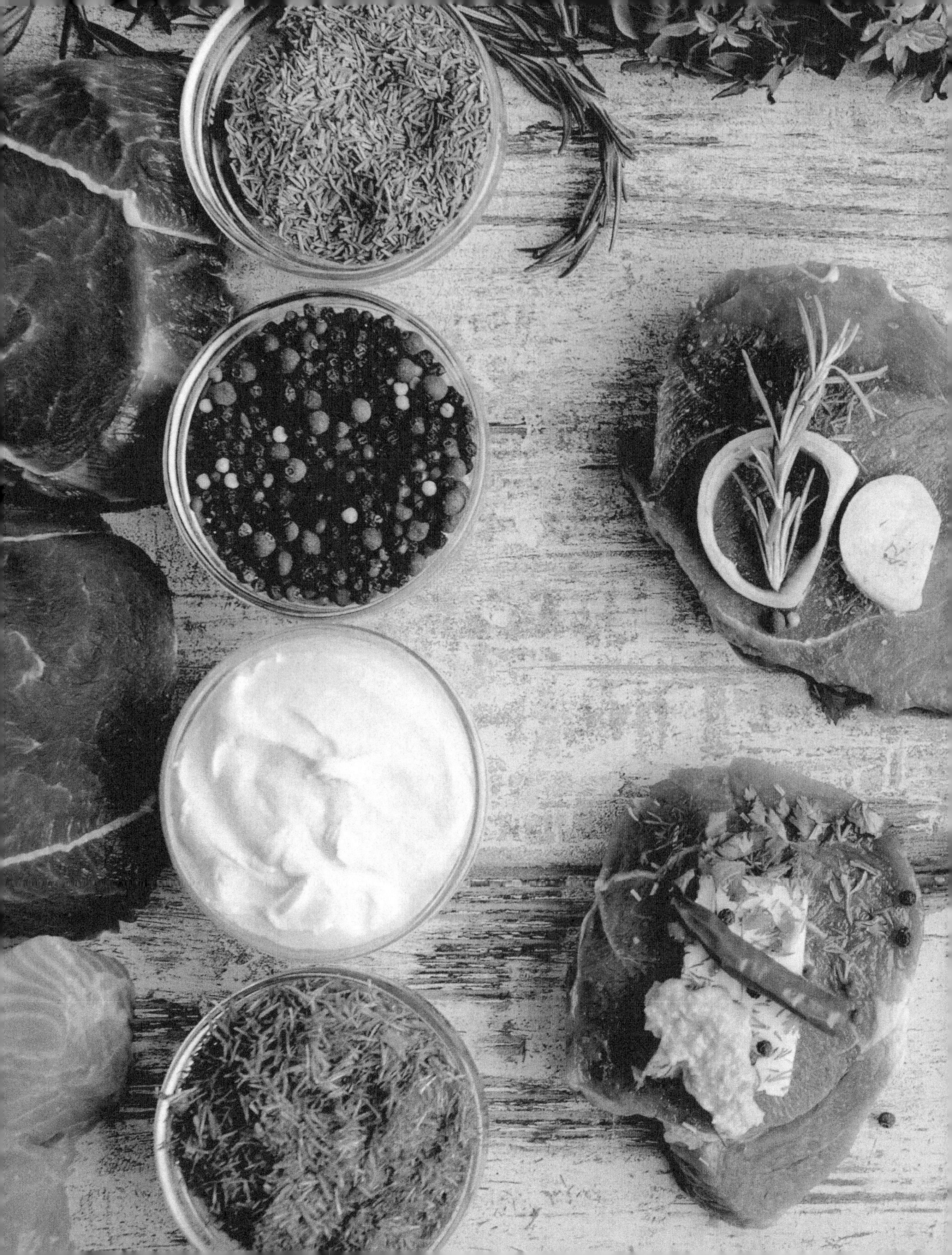

CHAPTER

2

How to Cook
Sous Vide

Getting Set Up

Learning the Controls
Each sous vide circulator is a little different, but there are two main types: those with a display and a temperature control, and others which are controlled via a Bluetooth connection and a smartphone app. Since timing isn't as big a concern with sous vide as with other types of cooking, many circulators do not have a timer control, which is not a problem. Simply set your circulator to the correct temperature and wait for the heating element to bring the water to temperature.

The Cooking Process
Sous vide cooking uses precise heat to bring your food to the correct internal temperature. This gentle cooking process may take a little longer than conventional cooking depending on what you are cooking, but on the plus side, you won't screw it up. A typical steak will cook for about one hour in the water bath before it is ready to be seared. While it may take a little longer, you will have a steak which is perfectly pink all the way through, rather than having a steak which has a little pink and a lot of grey because of your lack of cooking skills.

1 Place your Everie container on a level surface which is close enough to a grounded power outlet. Insert your sous vide circulator into the hole at the corner of the Everie's lid and attach to the lip of the container.

2 Fill the container to between six and ten quarts of water depending on what you intend to cook. Your food needs to be completely submerged in the water by several inches to cook evenly. Set to your desired temperature and wait until the water has reached the correct temperature.

3 Place the food you want to cook in either zipperlock bags or vacuum seal bags. Remove all of the air from the bags.

4 Place the bags of food into the water bath and make sure they are completely submerged. Follow the recipe to determine how long the food should cook and set a timer.

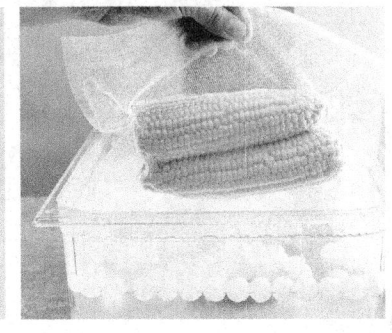

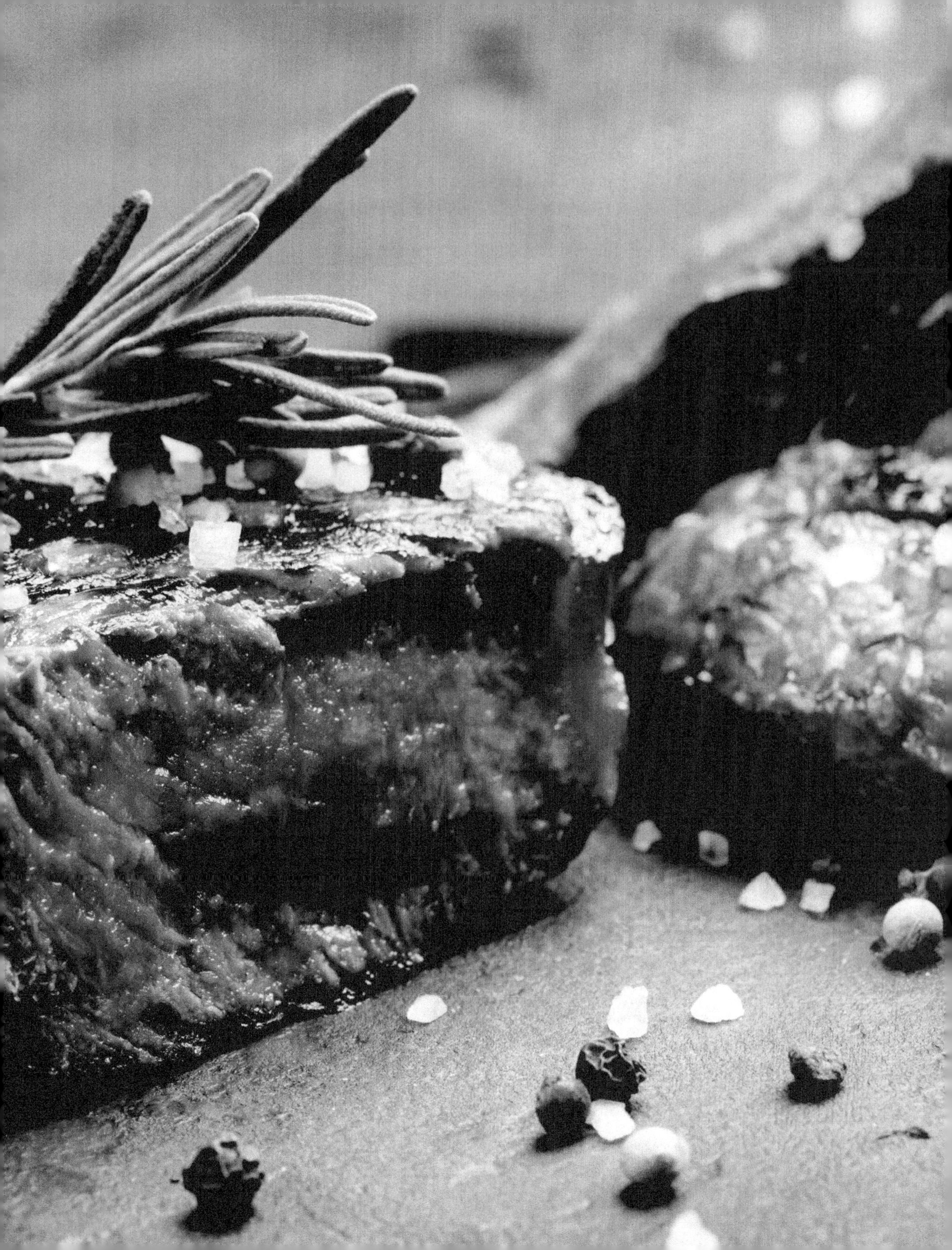

Workarounds

The water in your sous vide container is constantly moving because the sous vide circulator has a motor which keeps the water moving. As a result, you may find that your food has a tendency to move around in the container. This can be a problem because you do not want your food to come into contact with the circulator and possibly clog its vents. To keep you food in place, use small metal butterfly clips to attach the bag to the edge of the container. This will keep your food in place and safely away from the circulator.

If you are cooking for long periods of time and using vacuum sealed bags to hold your food, you may find that after twenty-four to thirty hours the seal begins to weaken and air is let into the bag. This is because long cooks require higher heat, and this heat can wear out the vacuum seal. A great way to remedy this is to double seal your bags. Simply vacuum seal normally, and then add another seal a couple of centimeters from the first seal. The addition of the extra seal should keep your bags airtight for the remainder of the cook.

Many sous vide recipes advise you to set your sous vide circulator to the exact temperature you would like your food to end up at. While this can be a great recommendation for fish, eggs, and vegetables, it may cause other foods like steaks and chops to come out overcooked. When you finish cooking a steak sous vide, you will most likely want to sear it to achieve a nice brown crust. Since it will take a couple of minutes of high heat cooking in a pan or on a grill to produce this result, you will end up raising the temperature of the meat. To avoid overcooking, set your sous vide circulator lower than your desired internal temperature by five degrees. So if you want a nice medium rare steak cooked to 130°F. Set your sous vide circulator to 125°F and the searing should bring it right up to 130°F.

10 Minute Quick-Start

Your First Steak Dinner

Getting perfect results with a nice steak can be difficult. You have to know exactly what temperature the inside of the steak will be, and there are so many variables. Luckily, cooking steaks sous vide takes most of the guesswork out of it. Now you don't have to rely on pressing your thumb into the meat to try and estimate how well done it is. All you have to do is set your sous vide to your desired temperature and get ready for an amazing dinner.

1 Collect These Ingredients:

- 2 12 oz. New York strip steaks
- 1 lb. fresh asparagus
- 1 tablespoon olive oil
- 2 tablespoons vegetable oil
- 1 tablespoon butter
- Salt and black pepper

2 Collect These Tools:

- Sous vide container
- Sous vide circulator
- Zipperlock or vacuum seal bags
- Tongs
- Cast iron pan or grill

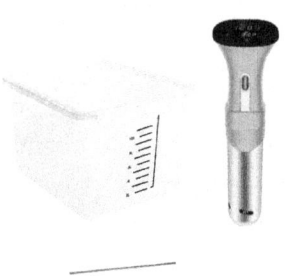

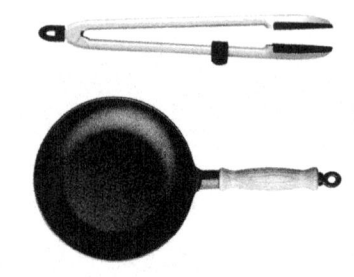

The goal of "10 Minute Quick-Start" is to walk you through making your first meal so you "learn by doing" in under 10 minutes. Even if you've never cooked sous vide or you've tried and failed miserably, this quick start guide is going to make sure you stop sucking at sous vide right now.

3 Follow These Steps:

1. Fill your sous vide container with water and attach the sous vide circulator. Set the circulator to 125F for medium rare steaks and 130F for medium.
2. Season the steaks with a generous amount of salt and place into zipperlock or vacuum seal bags and remove air.
3. Place the asparagus in a zipperlock or vacuum seal bag and add a little salt and one tablespoon of olive oil. Remove air and seal the bag.
4. When the water bath reaches the proper temperature, place the bags with the steak in the water. Allow to cook for one to two hours.
5. When half an hour is remaining for the steaks, add the bag with the asparagus to the water bath.
6. When the steaks are nearly finished cooking, heat a cast iron pan over high heat and add two tablespoons of vegetable oil. When the oil is just starting to smoke, remove the steaks from their bags, sprinkle with pepper and add to the pan. Cook the steaks for two minutes, flip and add the butter to the pan, spooning it over the steaks. Remove the steaks from the pan and allow to sit for a couple of minutes.
7. Remove the asparagus from the bag and divide onto two plates. You can serve the steaks whole or slice to serve.

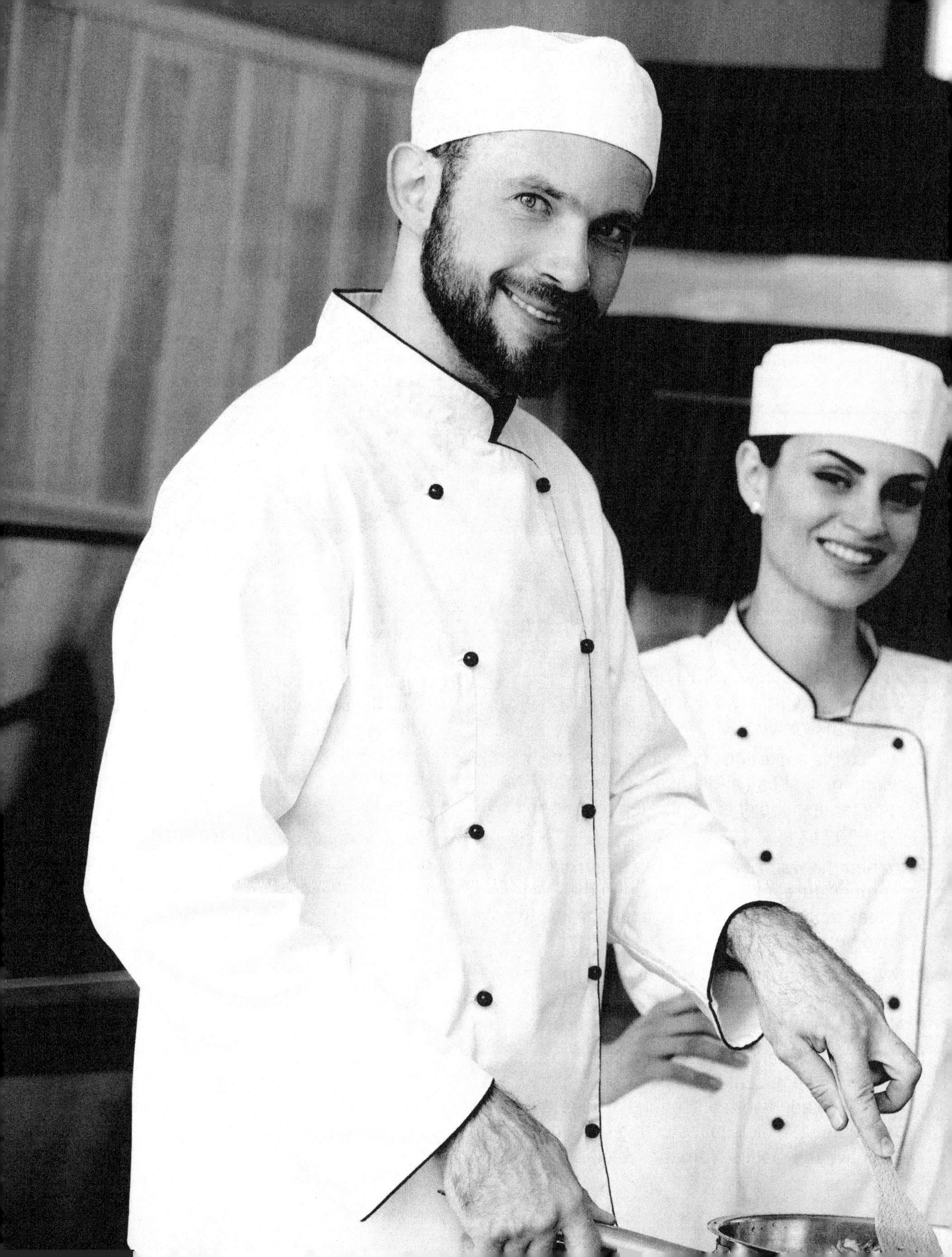

CHAPTER 3

Pro Tips

A Great Sear Is Another Way To Add Flavor

You've used your sous vide to cook your food to the desired temperature, but what's next? Well, certain foods like vegetables and fish are often ready to eat right out of the bag. But things like beef or chicken can benefit from one more step. If you're making a nice New York Strip steak, your sous vide has cooked the inside to whatever temperature you prefer, but most of us like a nice dark sear on a steak. Once you're happy with the internal temperature, heat a pan (preferably a cast iron pan) to the point of smoking and add a tablespoon of vegetable oil. Drop your steak in the pan for just a couple of minutes on each side to achieve a nice dark sear. To enhance the sear further, try putting a tablespoon of butter in the pan while searing for an even darker, crisper crust. The high heat will sear the outside nicely, but the inside will stay juicy and rare.

With Sous Vide There's No Need To Rest Meat

One of the dumbest mistakes you can make is not letting meat rest after cooking. You lose all of the juice and your meat is dry. Luckily, with sous vide cooking you don't really need to rest. Depending on how large a piece of meat you have, resting time could range anywhere from ten minutes for an average steak, to about an hour for a rib roast. The reason meat needs to rest is to give the cooler internal temperature of the meat time to even out with the hotter external temperature of the surface of the meat. Allowing the meat to rest ensures that the juices within the meat will be fully absorbed and not lost when the meat is cut. When meat is cooked sous vide, this difference between the internal and external temperatures does not exist, which means meat cooked sous vide can be served right out of the bag. Or right out of the pan if you're searing it.

Cook Low And Slow For Fall-Off-the-Bone Meats

Meats like pork shoulder and brisket are delicious, but in order to get that fall off the bone texture they have to be cooked for a long time. This means that you either have to smoke them at low temperatures or keep them in the oven all day. This can be tricky if you have no idea what you are doing. But with sous vide cooking you can safely cook food all day without setting the house on fire or, worse yet, making terrible, chewy meat. If you want to make perfect fall of the bone meats at home, season the outside of the meat with your favorite rub, seal it, and adjust your sous vide to 165 degrees. Then submerge the meat in the water and cook for twelve hours for tender ribs or twenty-four hours for brisket.

Never Cook Too Low For Too Long

Sous vide cooking is one of the easiest and safest ways to cook almost anything, but if food is cooked at too low a temperature for too long, you run the risk of killing people and we don't want you to kill people. Foods like fish are best at around 120-125 degrees, but they only require around a half an hour in the sous vide to cook properly. After more than three hours at such a low temperature, bacteria can begin to multiply and become a health risk. A good rule of thumb is: Foods that are best at a low temperature like fish should only cook for a short time (less than three hours), and foods that need a long cook time need to be cooked at high temperatures (165 degrees and up). If you stick to these basic guidelines your food will always be 100% safe to eat and you won't kill anyone.

How to Properly Season Meats

We've already discussed how and why sous vide is such a great method for making perfectly cooked food, but if you really want to get the most out of the experience, seasoning in the bag is the way to go. If you preseason your food, the vacuum seal will press those delicious flavors right into the food and keep them there for the entire cooking time. Not sure about reapplying seasoning or basting? Don't worry about it! By cooking sous vide you can be assured that your seasonings will stick and remain evenly distributed without any extra work. To enhance the flavor of things like chicken breast even more, you can add a couple of tablespoons of olive oil to the bag to create the most tender chicken you've ever had. If you're using your sous vide to make barbecued meats, a couple of drops of liquid smoke in the bag will simulate that distinctive wood smoke flavor without the risk of starting a fire.

If you keep in mind what we've talked about, you can cook your favorite foods, confident that you no longer suck at sous vide.

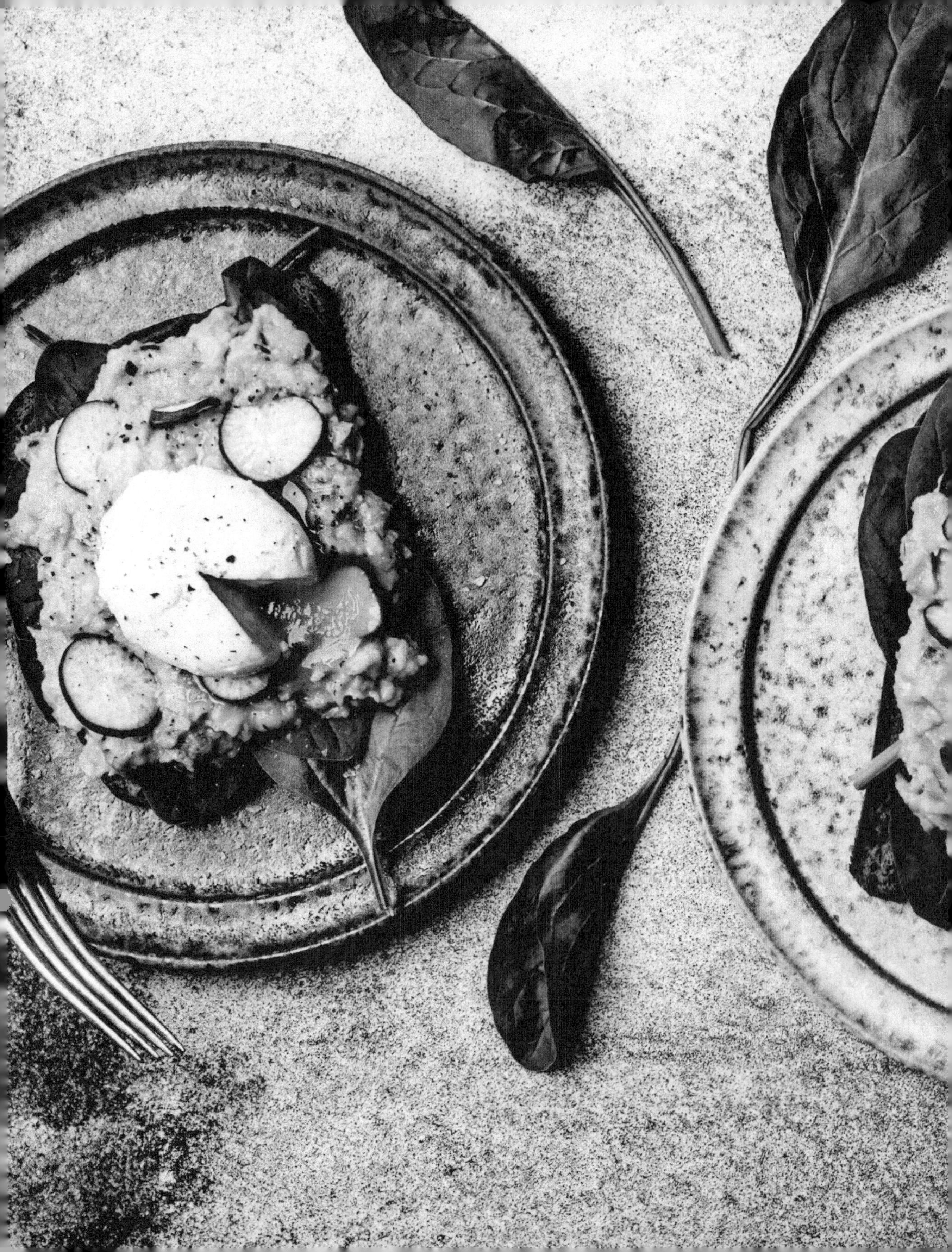

CHAPTER 4

Breakfast
Dishes

Hearty Sous Vide Pumpkin Bread

Hearty pumpkin bread is just the way to make the most out of your Everie when it comes to serving a lush breakfast or brunch.

Servings: 4
Prep time: 15 minutes
Cook time: 3 hours

1 cup unbleached flour
2 teaspoons ground cinnamon
1 teaspoon baking powder
1/2 teaspoon ground nutmeg
1/4 teaspoon baking soda
1/8 teaspoon ground cloves
3/4 cup canned pumpkin puree
1/2 cup vegetable oil
1/3 cup sugar
1/4 cup dark brown sugar, packed
1/2 teaspoon sea salt
2 large eggs
4 (8 ounce) mason jars
Butter, for greasing

1. Preheat sous vide water bath to 195°F.
2. Grease 4 (8 ounce) mason jars with butter.
3. Whisk together flour, cinnamon, baking powder, nutmeg, baking soda, and cloves in a medium mixing bowl.
4. Whisk together pumpkin, vegetable oil, sugars, and salt until well combined in a separate mixing bowl; add eggs one at a time until well combined.
5. Fold flour mixture into pumpkin mixture until just combined.
6. Divide the batter between the prepared mason jars; no more than 2/3 full.
7. Firmly tap jars on the counter to remove air bubbles and seal lids until just tight.
8. Add jars to water bath and cook for 3 hours.
9. Transfer to a cooling rack.
10. Remove the lids and let the bread cool to room temperature.
11. Slice and serve!

Nutrition

Calories: 534 Sodium: 376 mg, Dietary Fiber: 2.9g, Fat: 33.2g, Carbs: 55g, Protein: 7g

Perfect Eggs
with Avocado Toast

Creamy avocado spread on toast is a healthy and delicious way to start your day - especially served with decadent poached eggs!

Servings: 2
Prep time: 10 minutes
Cook time: 1 hour 5 minutes

4 eggs
4 slices bread
1 ripe avocado
Sea salt, to taste
Black pepper, to taste
Chili threads, for garnish

1. Preheat sous vide water bath to 145°F.
2. Gently lower eggs into the water bath and cook for 1 hour.
3. Toast bread until golden brown in a toaster or oven.
4. Remove eggs and open over toast.
5. Garnish with salt, pepper, and chili threads to serve!

Nutrition

Calories: 388 Sodium: 411 mg, Dietary Fiber: 7.5g, Fat: 29.4g, Carbs: 19.4g, Protein: 14.8g

Cinnamon
French Toast

Fluffy and decadent this breakfast bread is best topped with powdered sugar and maple syrup.

Servings: 4
Prep time: 5 minutes
Cook time: 1 hour

4 slices French bread
2 eggs
1/2 cup heavy cream
1 teaspoon vanilla extract
1 teaspoon cinnamon
2 teaspoons vegetable oil or shortening
Powdered sugar, for serving
Maple syrup, for serving

1. Preheat sous vide to 147°F.
2. Whisk together eggs, cream, vanilla, and cinnamon in a bowl.
3. Dredge bread slices in the cream mixture.
4. Add bread to a vacuum bag and seal.
5. Cook for 1 hour.
6. Add oil to a large frying pan and heat to medium-high.
7. Remove French toast from sous vide and brown on both sides for 2 minutes.
8. Serve with powdered sugar and syrup.

Nutrition
Calories: 221 Sodium: 245 mg, Dietary Fiber: 1.1g, Fat: 10.6g, Carbs: 24.6g, Protein: 6.9g

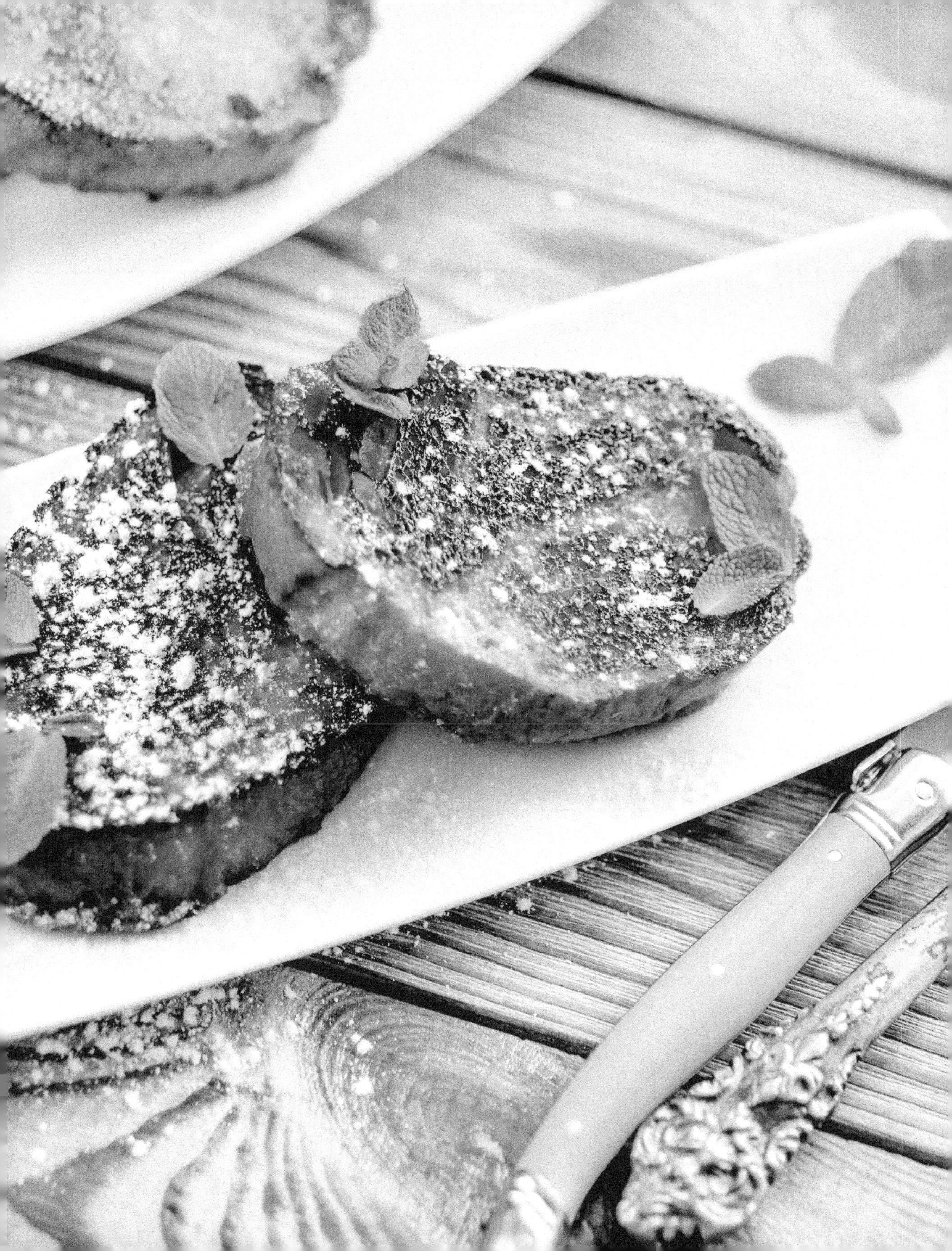

Asparagus & Feta Flan

Bright, earthy asparagus meets decadent feta cheese for a flavor explosion that will turn ordinary breakfast into something out of this world.

Servings: 4
Prep time: 15 minutes
Cook time: 45 minutes

½ tablespoon olive oil
1 small onion, peeled and diced
½ teaspoon melted butter
4 eggs
½ cup heavy cream
1 teaspoon chives, chopped
4 asparagus tips, cut in half lengthwise
¼ cup feta cheese, crumbled
Sea salt and pepper, to taste

1. Place a baking rack in the Everie and fill with water.
2. Grease each ramekin with the melted butter.
3. Preheat sous vide water bath to 185°F.
4. Heat the olive oil in a medium sized saucepan.
5. Add the diced onions and sauté until soft and golden about 10 minutes; set aside to cool.
6. Add the eggs and cream to a bowl, add a pinch of salt and pepper, and the chopped chives and whisk until well combined.
7. Divide the onions among the ramekins and pour the egg mixture on top of the onions.
8. Top each with the sliced asparagus tips and feta.
9. Carefully place the ramekins into the water oven on the raised baking rack; do not get any water into the ramekins.
10. Cover the ramekins with squares of tented foil to prevent condensation from dripping into them.
11. Cook for 45 minutes.
12. Remove and allow to cool for 5 minutes and serve!

Nutrition
Calories: 168 Sodium: 293 mg, Dietary Fiber: 0.7g, Fat: 14.2g, Carbs: 3.3g, Protein: 7.7g

Sous Vide
Overnight Oatmeal

Overnight oats are hearty and delicious when whipped up in your sous vide, and you'll have one healthy meal with minimal effort when you cook these for breakfast while you sleep.

Servings: 2
Prep time: 10 minutes
Cook time: 10 hours

- 2/3 cup rolled oats
- 2/3 cup milk
- 1 cup water
- 2 teaspoons raisins, divided
- 2 teaspoons sunflower seeds, divided
- 2 teaspoons honey, divided
- 2 (8 ounce) mason jars

1. Preheat sous vide water bath to 140°F.
2. Divide the oats and milk between the two jars and top up each with a half cup of water.
3. Add 1 teaspoon raisins, sunflower seeds, and honey to each and firmly screw the lids on.
4. Submerge the jars in the water bath, and cook overnight for about 10 hours.
5. Open and eat straight from the jar!

Nutrition
Calories: 180 Sodium: 44 mg, Dietary Fiber: 3g, Fat: 4g, Carbs: 30.8g, Protein: 6.6g

Soft Poached Eggs
In Hashbrown Nests

One of my absolute favorites, these delicious little eggs are wrapped in hashbrowns for one savory breakfast treat!

Servings: 6
Prep time: 10 minutes
Cook time: 1 hour

Ingredients:
- 12 large eggs, at room temperature
- Olive oil non-stick cooking spray
- 6 cups frozen shredded hashbrowns, fully thawed
- 3 tablespoons extra-virgin olive oil
- 1 teaspoon sea salt
- 1 teaspoon black pepper

1. Preheat sous vide water bath to 145°F.
2. Gently lower eggs into the water bath and cook for 1 hour.
3. Preheat an oven to 375.
4. Generously coat 12 cup muffin pan with cooking spray.
5. Squeeze potatoes in a cheese cloth or paper towel very well, over the sink, to remove as much liquid as possible.
6. Transfer to a large bowl and stir in oil, salt, and pepper to combine.
7. Divide the mixture among the muffin cups; filling no more than 1/3 full.
8. Press hashbrowns into the bottom and up the sides of each cup to form a "nest."
9. Bake the hashbrown nests until golden brown on the bottom and edges, about 30 minutes.
10. Let the nests cool in the pan for 5 minutes.
11. Remove nests to plate, crack two sous vide cooked eggs into each nest, sprinkle with more salt and pepper to serve!

Nutrition

Calories: 617 Sodium: 986 mg, Dietary Fiber: 5.1g, Fat: 36.5g, Carbs: 55.8g, Protein: 17.3g

Egg Yolk Croquette

A Vegetarian version of the Scotch Egg, these delicious eggs are best served on a bed of arugula for one decadent morning meal.

Servings: 3
Prep time: 5 minutes
Cook time: 55 minutes

6 egg yolks
1 cup panko bread crumbs
1 cup flour
1 teaspoon sea salt
1 teaspoon black pepper
2 cups vegetable oil
Hollandaise sauce, for serving
Arugula, for serving

For the egg wash:
1 egg
1 teaspoon whole milk

1. Preheat sous vide water bath to 148°F.
2. Add egg yolks to a resealable bag, seal, and gently place eggs in the water bath: make sure the water completely covers the eggs.
3. Cook for 45 minutes.
4. Mix panko, flour, salt, and pepper together in a large mixing bowl and set aside.
5. Combine egg wash ingredients with a whisk until well-combined in a separate bowl.
6. Remove yolks from sous vide.
7. Gently dredge egg yolks in egg wash then roll in panko mix.
8. Heat vegetable oil in a frying pan to high heat.
9. Fry croquettes on each side for 30 second until golden brown; do not fry more than 2 minutes.
10. Serve on a bed of arugula topped with sous vide hollandaise sauce from the recipes below!

Nutrition
Calories: 1732 Sodium: 1075 mg, Dietary Fiber: 3.1g, Fat: 158.8g, Carbs: 63.2g, Protein: 17.4g

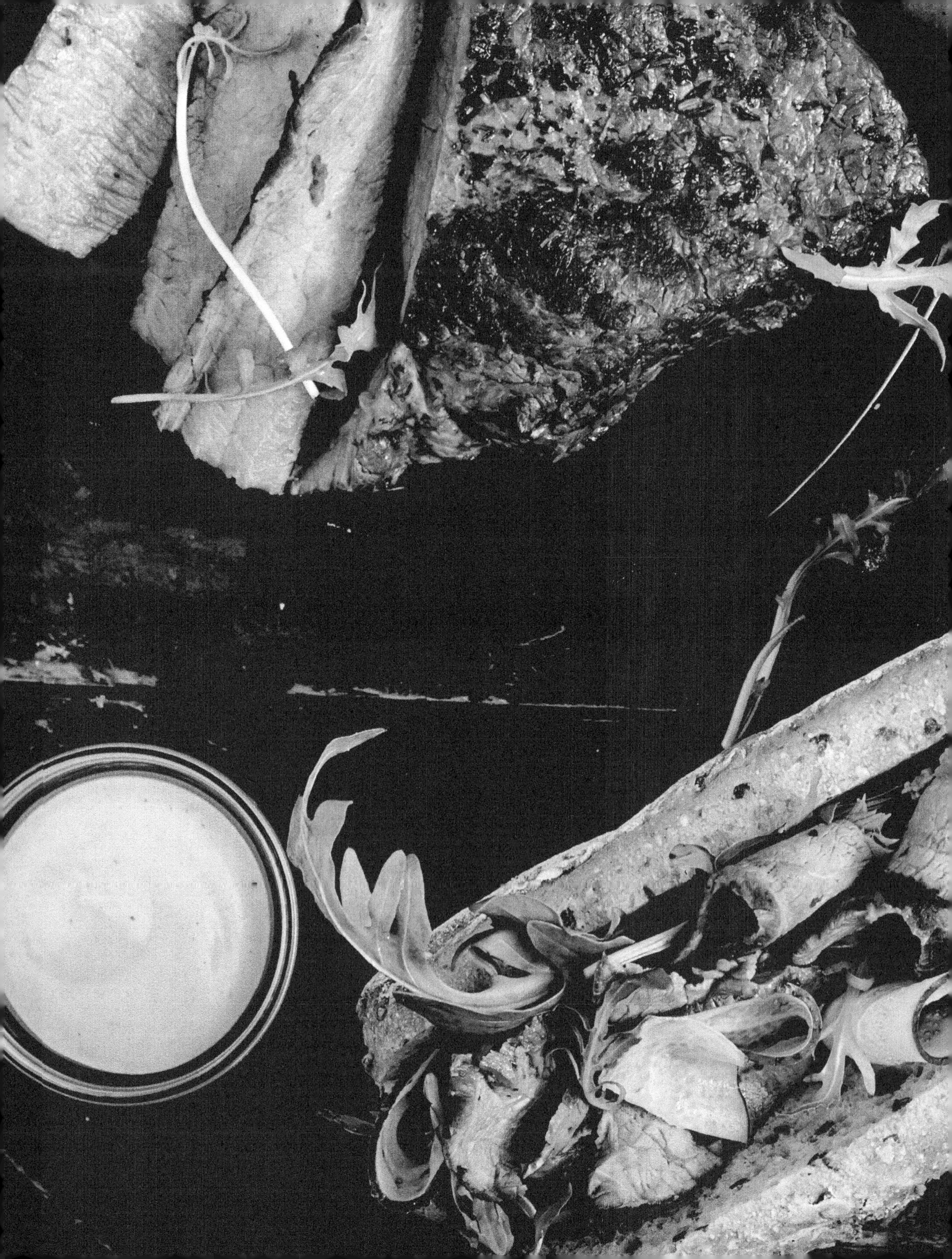

CHAPTER

5

Main Dishes
Beef & Lamb

Juicy French Dip Sandwiches

French dip sandwiches are the perfect lunchtime meal to whip up in your Everie sous vide!

Servings: 6 - 8
Prep time: 5 minutes
Cook time: 30 hours

3 lbs. beef top round roast
1 teaspoon salt, plus more to taste
1/4 teaspoon black pepper, plus more to taste
1 tablespoon grapeseed oil
1/2 cup red wine, like Bordeaux
2 cups low-sodium beef broth
1 bay leaf

For sandwiches:

1 large yellow onion, thinly sliced
6 to 8 French rolls or hoagie buns
Sliced provolone cheese, optional

1. Bring a large frying pan to medium-high heat with grapeseed oil.
2. Season meat liberally with salt and pepper.
3. Sear for 3 minutes on each side.
4. Preheat sous vide bath to 131°F.
5. Add roast to a vacuum bag with red wine, beef broth, and bay leaf, and cook for 30 hours.
6. Strain juice from bag to serve with the sandwiches.
7. Trim the beef in thin slices.
8. Assemble the sandwiches: meat slices, top with cheese and onion, then top bun. Serve with a ramekin of au jus and enjoy!

Nutrition

Calories: 161 Sodium: 830 mg, Dietary Fiber: 1.4g, Fat: 5g, Carbs: 17.1g, Protein: 9.2g

Awesome Burgers

Juicy burgers are just as easy to make in your Everie - just be sure to serve them classic style with a side of fries and a big kosher pickle.

Servings: 4 - 6
Prep time: 5 minutes
Cook time: 1 hour

1 lb. grass fed ground beef
Sea salt, to taste
Black pepper, to taste

1. Preheat a sous vide water bath to 135°F.
2. Salt and pepper the ground beef.
3. Form the ground beef into 4 (1 and ½ inch thick) patties.
4. Place burgers in a single layer in a large vacuum bag and seal.
5. Cook for 1 hour.
6. Remove and sear in a frying pan, on medium high heat, for 1 minute on each side.
7. Serve with your favorite buns and toppings.

Nutrition

Calories: 533 Sodium: 239 mg, Dietary Fiber: 0g, Fat: 29.3g, Carbs: 0g, Protein: 61.3g

Tenderest Steak
& Buttery Potatoes

A beautifully basic meal, this recipe helps you add some succulent flavor to your favorite meat and potatoes.

Servings: 2
Prep time: 10 minutes
Cook time: 1 hour 45 minutes

2 (12 ounce) strip steaks
6 garlic cloves
6 sprigs of thyme
1 pound baby potatoes
½ cup sweet onion, thin sliced
1 ounce of unsalted butter
Kosher salt, to taste
Cracked pepper, to taste

1. Preheat your sous vide machine in a large pot of water to 133°F
2. Season 2 strip steaks on both sides with salt and pepper and transfer to a vacuum bag along with garlic and thyme.
3. Seal airtight and set aside.
4. Add the potatoes, onions, butter, and salt and pepper to a separate vacuum bag and seal airtight.
5. Cook potatoes for 45 minutes.
6. Add the steak and cook both for 1 additional hour.
7. Brown steak in a frying pan on both sides for 1 minute.
8. Slice the steak and serve alongside the buttered potatoes.

Nutrition
Calories: 2164 Sodium: 859 mg, Dietary Fiber: 7.6g, Fat: 75.7g, Carbs: 35.8g, Protein: 316.9g

Savory Pastrami

Delicate pastrami is the perfect way to master your Everie and make some yummy sandwiches like the Reuben on rye bread.

Servings: 10
Prep time: 24 hours
Cook time: 48 hours

8 lb. beef brisket

For the brine:

2 quarts water
1 cup kosher salt
1 tablespoon caraway seeds
1 tablespoon dill seeds
1 teaspoon coriander seeds
2 tablespoons black pepper
1 tablespoon allspice berries
½ teaspoon clove
1 teaspoon liquid smoke
4 bay leaves
2 teaspoons cracked black pepper

For the rub:

Cracked black pepper

1. Bring two quarts of water to a boil.
2. Mix in all of the brining ingredients until the sugar and salt are completely dissolved in the water.
3. Remove from heat and add 3 cups of ice to cool the brine.
4. Place the brisket in a 2-gallon zip lock bag, add the brine, seal and place in the refrigerator for 24 hours; flip the meat 12 hours in to ensure total brining.
5. Remove the brisket from the bag and wash it thoroughly under cold water. Remove as much of the brine as possible.
6. Preheat a sous vide bath to 140°F.
7. Liberally coat the brisket with cracked pepper, and place in a vacuum bag.
8. Seal and cook for 48 hours.
9. Remove the brisket from the sous vide bath and allow it to cool while in the bag.
10. Remove from bag when brisket is slightly warm to the touch.
11. Trim, slice, and serve any way you like!

Nutrition

Calories: 684 Sodium: 11564 mg, Dietary Fiber: 1g, Fat: 22.9g, Carbs: 2.2g, Protein: 110.5g

Succulent
Spaghetti and Meatballs

A dinner staple in most homes, this sous vide recipe helps you whip up something hearty any night of the week.

Servings: 4
Prep time: 15 minutes
Cook time: 2 hrs 10 minutes

- 1 lb. ground pork
- 1 lb. ground beef
- 1 egg
- 1/2 cup Italian bread crumbs
- 1 medium yellow onion, minced fine
- 2 cloves of garlic, minced fine
- 2 sprigs of fresh oregano, chopped fine
- 1 can stewed tomatoes, mashed well
- Olive oil
- Sea salt
- Black pepper
- 1 package spaghetti pasta
- Shaved parmesan, for garnish

1. Preheat a sous vide bath to 140°F.
2. Combine pork, beef, egg, bread crumbs, half the onion, half the garlic, and salt and pepper to taste, in a mixing bowl until well-combined.
3. Form 8 meatballs, 2 inches wide, with your hands or a small ice cream scoop.
4. Heat a large saucepan over high heat and add a tablespoon of olive oil.
5. Sear meatballs on all sides; set aside.
6. Drain the pan and add the remaining onion.
7. Stir in remaining garlic, the tomatoes and juice from the can.
8. Salt to taste.
9. Mix well and simmer for 5 minutes.
10. Turn off heat and let cool 5 minutes.
11. Combine meatballs and sauce in a large vacuum bag and seal.
12. Sous vide for 2 hours.
13. Prepare spaghetti according to package instructions.
14. Top with meatballs and sauce, and garnish with parmesan to serve.

Nutrition

Calories: 530 Sodium: 636 mg, Dietary Fiber: 3.2g, Fat: 17.9g, Carbs: 19.8g, Protein: 69.4g

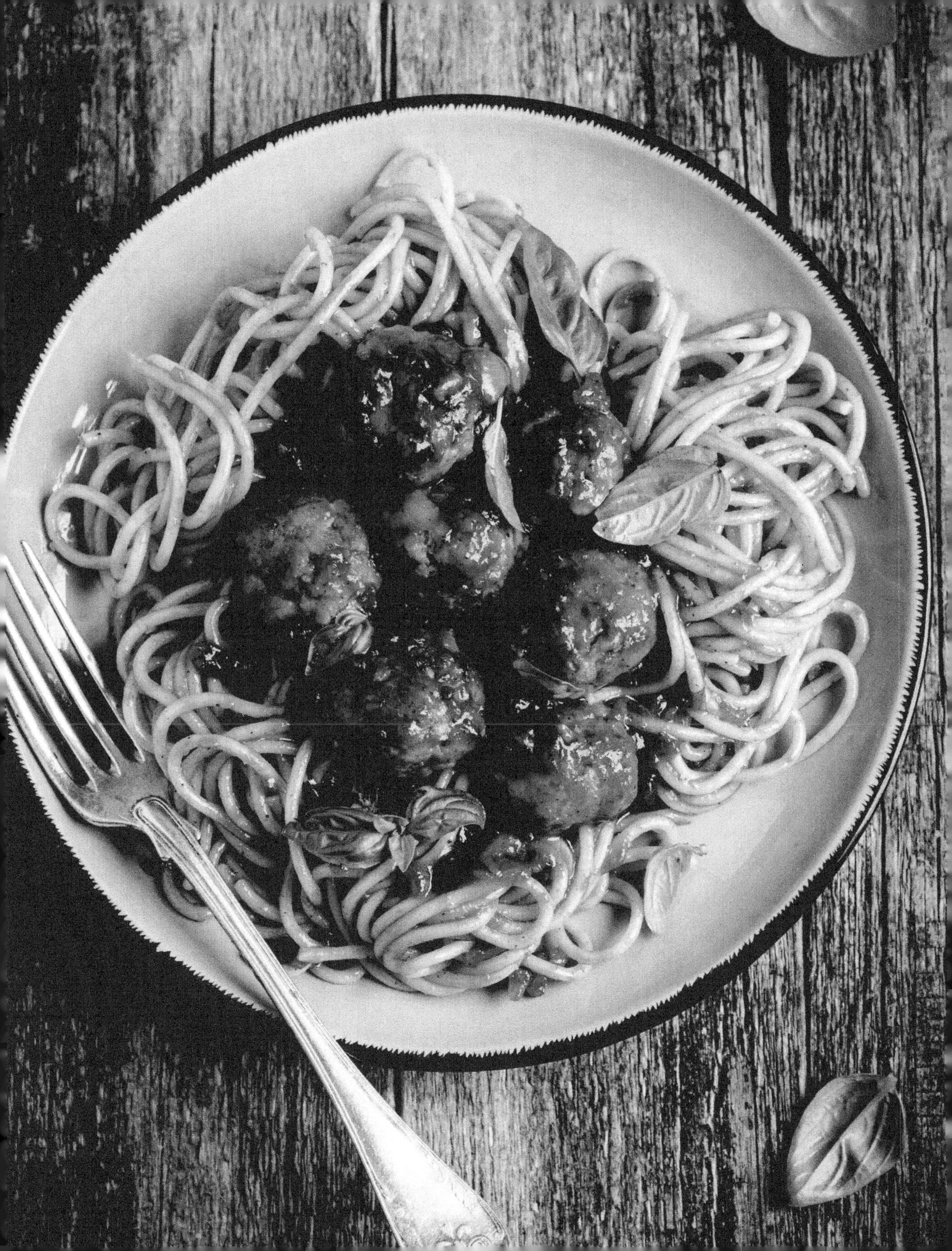

Sous Vide
Flat Iron Steak

Flat iron steak cooks up to delicious perfection when you use your sous vide to prepare it in no time.

Servings: 4
Prep time: 5 minutes
Cook time: 12 hours

2 (10 ounce) flat iron steaks
Cracked black pepper
Sea salt
Premium olive oil, like Partanna
Steak sauce, for serving

1. Preheat sous vide water bath to 130°F for medium-rare.
2. Coat steaks evenly on both sides with salt and pepper.
3. Add steaks to a vacuum bag, not overlapping one another, seal, and cook 12 hours.
4. Add olive oil to a large frying pan on medium-high heat.
5. Remove steaks from sous vide and sear on both sides for 1 minute each.
6. Serve with steak sauce and your favorite side dishes!

Nutrition
Calories: 2352 Sodium: 887 mg, Dietary Fiber: 0g, Fat: 115g, Carbs: 0.8g, Protein: 310g

Sunday
Eye Of Round Roast

Whip up a full Sunday roast with this luxurious and easy sous vide eye of round!

Servings: 6
Prep time: 15 minutes
Cook time: 30 hours

3 lb. beef eye of round roast
Olive oil
1 1/2 tablespoons black pepper
1 1/2 tablespoons sea salt
3 cloves garlic, minced

1. Bring a large frying pan to medium-high heat with olive oil.
2. Season meat liberally with salt and pepper.
3. Sear for 3 minutes on each side.
4. Preheat sous vide bath to 131°F.
5. Add pot roast to a vacuum bag with minced garlic, and cook for 30 hours.
6. Trim, slice, and serve any way you like!

Nutrition
Calories: 272 Sodium: 1496 mg, Dietary Fiber: 0.5g, Fat: 9.6g, Carbs: 1.5g, Protein: 42.8g

Mouth-Watering Steak Sashimi with Ponzu Dressing

Melt in your mouth sashimi steak is dressed to impress your taste buds with this delicious recipe for ponzu - perfect for date night or a dinner party!

Servings: 2
Prep time: 10 minutes
Cook time: 1 hour 10 minutes

- 2 (1 inch thick) wagyu beef fillets
- 4 tablespoons grapeseed oil
- Sea salt, to taste

For the ponzu dressing:

- 1 tablespoon yuzu juice
- 1 tablespoon rice vinegar
- 1 tablespoon Japanese sake
- 1 teaspoon soy sauce

1. Preheat sous vide water bath to 130°F for medium-rare.
2. Coat steak evenly on both sides with sea salt.
3. Add steak to a vacuum bag, seal, and cook for 1 hour 10 minutes.
4. Combine all the ingredients for the ponzu dressing in a small bowl. Mix well and set aside.
5. Add grapeseed oil to a large frying pan on medium-high heat.
6. Transfer steak to a cutting board and slice into thin sashimi strips.
7. Serve hot with ponzu dipping sauce!

Nutrition

Calories: 406 Sodium: 812 mg, Dietary Fiber: 14.6g, Fat: 30.2g, Carbs: 17.5g, Protein: 12.2g

Juicy Beef Brisket

Take the effort out of juicy beef brisket when you cook it to perfection in your Everie sous vide style.

Servings: 6 - 8
Prep time: 5 minutes
Cook time: 36 hours

5 lb. beef brisket
Olive oil, for searing

For the rub:

1/3 cup coarse ground black peppercorns
1/4 cup kosher salt
1 tablespoon curing salt
1/4 teaspoon liquid smoke, like Colgin

1. Preheat a sous vide bath to 140°F
2. Combine the rub ingredients in a mixing bowl.
3. Liberally coat the brisket and place in a vacuum bag.
4. Seal and cook for 36 hours.
5. Remove the brisket from the sous vide bag and sear in olive oil on medium high for 5 minutes per side, until blackened.
6. Trim, slice, and serve any way you like!

Nutrition

Calories: 582 Sodium: 3969 mg, Dietary Fiber: 0.4g, Fat: 23.2g, Carbs: 1g, Protein: 86.7g

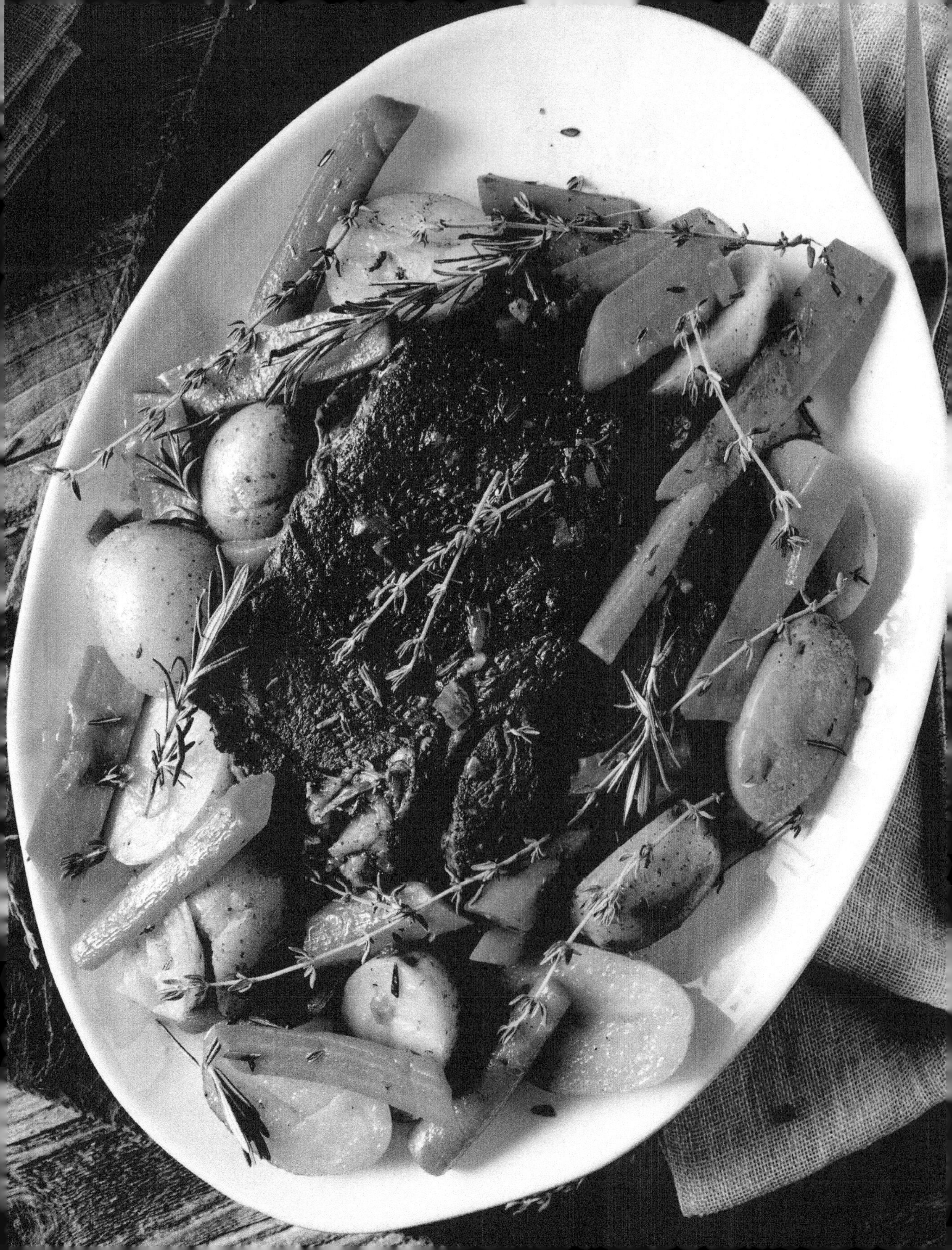

Slow-Cooked Pot Roast

One pot style meals are also just as easy to whip up for a hearty family meal when you sous vide.

Servings: 6 - 8
Prep time: 10 minutes
Cook time: 6 hours

2 lb. London broil
1 tablespoon sea salt
1 tablespoon black pepper
4 cups beef gravy, for serving

For the vegtables:

3 cups carrots, peeled and cut into large rounds
3 cups potatoes, peeled and cubed

1. Preheat the sous vide machine to 130°F.
2. Pat the sirloin tip roast dry using paper towels.
3. Season roast with salt and pepper on both sides, add to a vacuum bag and seal the bag.
4. Cook for 6 hours.
5. Add carrots and potatoes to a vacuum seal bag, season with pepper and salt, and cook for remaining 2 hours.
6. Remove and allow the roast to rest for 10 minutes.
7. Remove potatoes and carrots.
8. Carve roast and serve immediately with carrots and potatoes all topped with gravy.

Nutrition

Calories: 102 Sodium: 807 mg, Dietary Fiber: 2.6g, Fat: 1.8g, Carbs: 13.9g, Protein: 7.6g

Fragrant Beef Bourguignon

Hearty beef bourguignon is just the thing to cook up when you are craving a delicious comfort meal from the east of France.

Servings: 4
Prep time: 1 hour
Cook time: 16 hours

1 tablespoon olive oil
1 1/2 lbs. Beef chuck, cut into 1-inch cubes
1 1/2 teaspoon kosher salt, divided
½ teaspoon freshly ground black pepper
2 tablespoons cornstarch
2 carrots, diced
1 onion, sliced
2 teaspoons minced garlic
1 bottle dry French red wine, like Burgundy or Cote du Rhone
1 cup water
1 tablespoon beef bouillon
1 tablespoon tomato paste
1 bay leaf
2 cups cremini mushrooms, sliced thin
4 tablespoons unsalted butter at room temperature, divided
2 tablespoons all-purpose flour
1 teaspoon fresh thyme, chopped for garnish

Nutrition

Calories: 539 Sodium: 1038 mg, Dietary Fiber: 2.2g, Fat: 25.3g, Carbs: 16.5g, Protein: 53.8g

1. Set your sous vide to 140°F.
2. Combine 1 teaspoon salt, ground pepper, and cornstarch in a large mixing bowl.
3. Dry meat well with a paper towel, toss in salt mixture to coat very well.
4. Add olive oil to a large frying pan and heat to medium high.
5. Sear the beef, in batches, in the hot oil for 3 to 5 minutes, turning to brown on all sides.
6. Transfer to a vacuum bag.
7. Add the carrots and onions to the frying pan, cook 10 minutes, and add to vacuum bag.
8. Add the bottle of wine to the pan and deglaze over medium heat, scraping browned bits with a spatula.
9. Add the water and beef bouillon, bring to a simmer and reduce by about a quarter in volume, about 15 minutes.
10. Add the reduced wine mixture, tomato paste, thyme, and bay leaf to the bag.
11. Seal and cook for 16 hours.
12. Melt 2 tablespoons of butter in a separate frying pan and sauté mushrooms until softened, about 5 minutes; set aside.
13. Cut a small opening in the bag and pour the liquid into the frying pan.
14. Mash together the remaining 2 tablespoons of butter and the flour with a fork until it forms a paste.
15. Whisk paste into the sauce. Bring the sauce to a simmer, whisking often, and cook until the sauce is thick enough to coat a spoon.
16. Add the mushrooms, meat and vegetables to the sauce; toss to coat.
17. Garnish with fresh thyme and serve with a crusty loaf of French bread.

Sweet-Savory
Miso-Glazed Beef Steaks

Miso glaze adds a sweet flavor to your favorite BBQ beef steak for a flavor packed meal best served with brown rice and your favorite vegetables.

Servings: 4
Prep time: 8 hours
Cook time: 8 hours

2 (8 ounce) sirloin steaks
¼ cup miso paste
¼ cup brown sugar, packed
¼ cup soy sauce
¼ cup rice wine vinegar

1. Combine the miso, sugar, soy sauce, and rice wine in a food processor until smooth.
2. Marinate the steaks overnight in miso mixture.
3. Preheat a sous vide water bath to 150°F.
4. Add steaks in a single layer to a vacuum bag, seal and cook for 8 hours.
5. Heat a frying pan to medium-high heat.
6. Remove steaks from sous vide bath.
7. Sear the steaks in a frying pan for 1 minute on each side and serve.

Nutrition

Calories: 298 Sodium: 1617 mg, Dietary Fiber: 1.1g, Fat: 8.1g, Carbs: 14.7g, Protein: 37.4g

Satisfying Spicy
Corned Beef

Corned beef is a very versatile cut of meat that can be used to stuff sandwiches or even served as a one pot meal with cabbage, potatoes, and carrots.

Servings: 10
Prep time: 10 days
Cook time: 48 hours

7 lb. beef brisket, trimmed with some fat still remaining

For the brine:
2 quarts water
1 cup kosher salt
2 tablespoons curing salt
2 tablespoons honey
2 teaspoons cracked black pepper
½ cup brown sugar, packed
1 tablespoon dill seed
1 tablespoon star anise
1 cinnamon stick, chopped
1 teaspoon mustard seeds
1 tablespoon peppercorns
1/2 teaspoon mace
4 cloves garlic
2 Bay leaves
1 teaspoon garlic powder

For the rub:
3 tablespoons cracked black pepper
1/2 teaspoon chili powder
1/2 teaspoon garlic powder
1/2 teaspoon mustard seed

1. Bring two quarts of water to a boil.
2. Mix in all of the brining ingredients until the sugar and salt are completely dissolved in the water.
3. Remove from heat and add 2-3 pounds of ice to cool the brine.
4. Place the brisket into a 2-gallon zip lock bag, add the brine, seal and place in the refrigerator for 10 days.
5. Flip the meat over every day.
6. Remove the brisket from the bag and wash it thoroughly under cold water on day 10. Remove as much of the brine as possible.
7. Preheat a sous vide bath to 140°F.
8. Combine the rub ingredients in a mixing bowl.
9. Liberally coat the brisket and place in a vacuum bag.
10. Seal and cook for 48 hours.
11. Remove the corned beef from the sous vide bath and allow it to cool while in the bag
12. Remove from bag when corned beef is slightly warm to the touch.
13. Trim, slice, and serve any way you like!

Nutrition
Calories: 702 Sodium: 11925 mg, Dietary Fiber: 1g, Fat: 26.2g, Carbs: 13.2g, Protein: 97.7g

Melt-In-Your-Mouth Grilled Flank Steak

Delicious flank steak can be prepared in the sous vide for everything from stir fry to breakfast for dinner alongside eggs and toast.

Servings: 4
Prep time: 5 minutes
Cook time: 12 hours

1 (20 ounce) flank steak
1 teaspoon garlic powder
¼ teaspoon onion powder
¼ teaspoon ground black pepper
½ teaspoon sea salt
Premium olive oil, like Partanna
Flaky salt

1. Preheat sous vide water bath to 130°F for medium-rare.
2. Mix seasoning together in a small bowl and coat steak evenly on both sides.
3. Add steak to a vacuum bag, seal, and cook 12 hours.
4. Add olive oil to a large frying pan on medium-high heat.
5. Remove steak from sous vide and sear on both sides for 1 minute each.
6. Garnish with flaky salt and serve with your favorite sides!

Nutrition

Calories: 340 Sodium: 316 mg, Dietary Fiber: 1.1g, Fat: 14.9g, Carbs: 7.7g, Protein: 41.1g

Decadent Lamb Steak with Red Wine Sauce

Sous vide your lamb for an even more decadent, rich meal topped with red wine sauce and best served with roasted butternut squash and peas topped with pancetta.

Servings: 1 - 2
Prep time: 10 minutes
Cook time: 1 hour

1 lamb steak
1 tablespoon of butter
1 shallot, diced
2 cloves of garlic, minced
1 sprig of rosemary, removed from the stem and chopped
1/2 cup full-bodied red wine, like Merlot or Sangiovese
Salt and pepper, to taste

1. Preheat sous vide water bath to 135°F.
2. Season the lamb with salt and pepper and set aside.
3. Melt the first tablespoon of butter over medium-low heat in a frying pan.
4. Add the shallot, garlic, and rosemary, and cook until the shallots are soft and slightly caramelized, about 5 minutes.
5. Scrape everything into a large vacuum bag and set aside.
6. Turn pan to high heat and sear the steak for 2 minutes on each side until it has a light crust.
7. Use tongs to hold steak and sear the edges for 2 minutes each.
8. Transfer the steak to the vacuum bag.
9. Add the wine to the hot pan, scraping the browned fat up with a spatula, and let the wine reduce by half.
10. Add wine to vacuum bag and seal.
11. Cook for 1 hour.
12. Remove the steak from the bag.
13. Here, you can sear again or serve immediately with your favorite sous vide vegetables and sides!

Nutrition

Calories: 418 Sodium: 170 mg, Dietary Fiber: 0.8g, Fat: 18g, Carbs: 4.5g, Protein: 46.4g

Lamb Chops
with Basil Chimichurri

Decadent lamb chops topped with bright, fresh chimichurri is best served alongside roasted courgettes and leeks for one amazing meal any night of the week.

Servings: 4
Prep time: 10 minutes
Cook time: 2 hours

2 rack of lamb, frenched
2 cloves garlic, crushed
Sea salt
Black pepper
1 teaspoon olive oil, for searing

For the basil chimichurri:

1 cup fresh basil, finely chopped
1 shallot, chopped
1 clove of garlic, minced
1 teaspoon red chili flakes
1/3 cup olive oil
3 tablespoons red wine vinegar
1/4 teaspoon sea salt
1/4 teaspoon black pepper

1. Preheat sous vide water bath to 133°F.
2. Season lamb liberally with sea salt and pepper.
3. Add lamb, shallot, and garlic to vacuum bag, seal, and cook for 2 hours.
4. Combine the basil chimichurri ingredients in a large mixing bowl and stir until well-incorporated.
5. Cover and refrigerate until lamb is ready to plate.
6. Preheat a frying pan on medium high heat with olive oil.
7. Remove lamb chops, dry with a paper towel and sear for 2 minutes on each side.
8. Slice in between the bones, liberally top with basil chimichurri sauce, and enjoy.

Nutrition

Calories: 258 Sodium: 422 mg, Dietary Fiber: 0.2g, Fat: 23g, Carbs: 1.5g, Protein: 11.9g

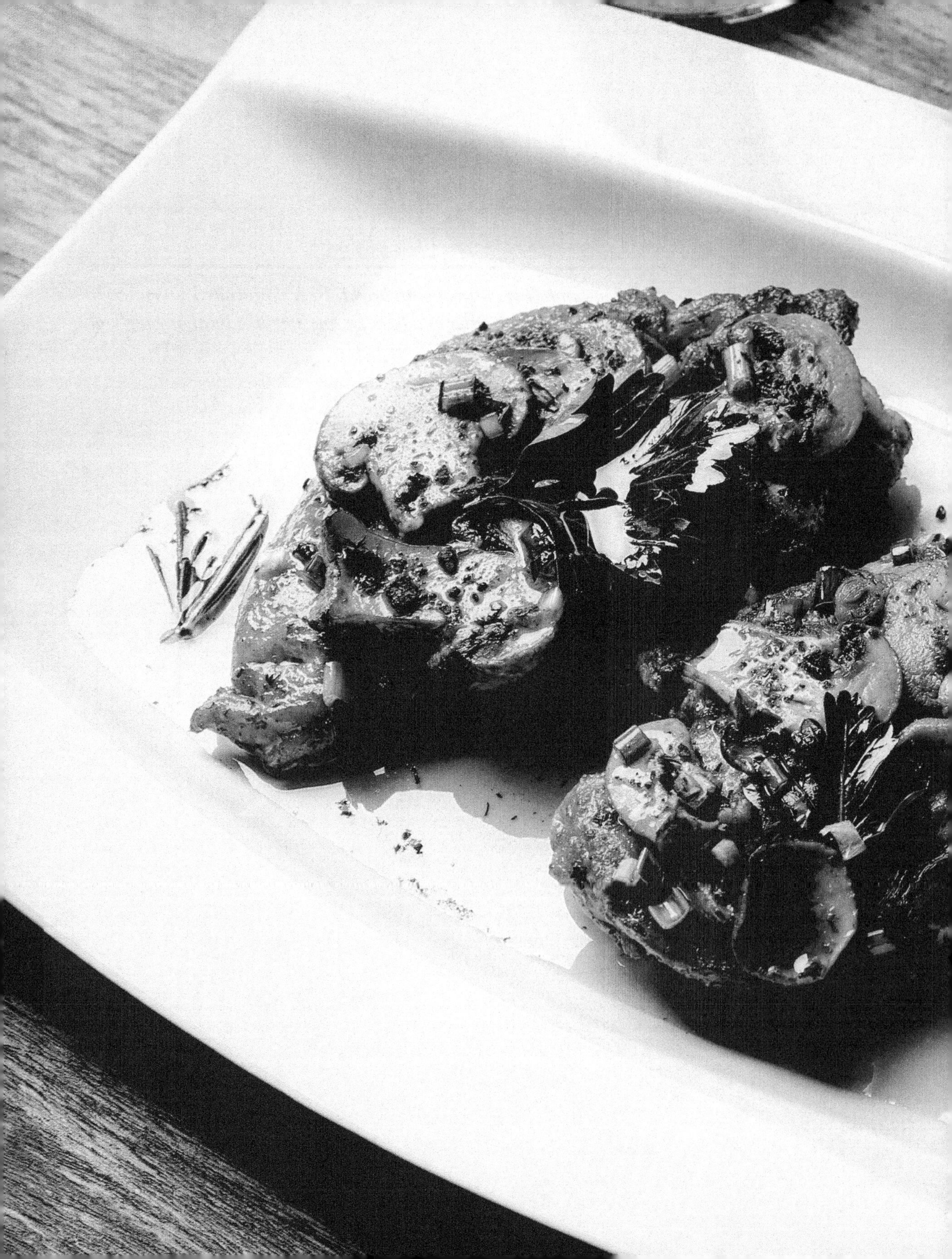

CHAPTER 6

Main Dishes
Poultry

Easy Chicken
Cordon Bleu

A taste of France is right at your fingertips with this delicious recipe, and you can easily whip up some sous vide asparagus and mashed potatoes to compliment this yummy dish!

Servings: 4
Prep time: 5 minutes
Cook time: 1 hour 30 minutes

- 2 boneless, skinless chicken breasts
- 1 teaspoon sea salt
- 1 teaspoon black pepper
- 4 swiss cheese slices
- 2 slices uncured ham, like Sam's Choice
- Activa meat glue, like Moo Glue

1. Prepare sous vide water bath to 140°F.
2. Butterfly chicken breasts and place them between two sheets of plastic wrap.
3. Tenderize flat using a meat tenderizer.
4. Remove plastic wrap and season the chicken with salt and pepper.
5. Lay swiss cheese in a single layer down the middle of each chicken breast.
6. Place a layer of uncured ham on top of the cheese.
7. Sprinkle sides of chicken breast with Activa and roll each chicken breast up like a jelly roll, beginning at the most narrow edge.
8. Place the chicken rolls in a vacuum bag, seal, and cook for 1 hour 30 minutes.
9. Allow chicken to rest for 5 minutes, and slice to serve warm!

Nutrition

Calories: 276 Sodium: 825 mg, Dietary Fiber: 0.1g, Fat: 14g, Carbs: 1.9g, Protein: 34.2g

Succulent Sous Vide Duck Breasts

Succulent duck breast cooks up in one easy recipe with your Everie sous vide!

Servings: 4
Prep time: 20 minutes
Cook time: 2 hrs 30 minutes

2 small duck breasts
¼ teaspoon sea salt
1 shallot, minced
1 teaspoon garlic, minced

1. Preheat a sous vide cooker water bath to 135°F.
2. Season duck with sea salt.
3. Add the duck breasts, shallots, and garlic to a vacuum bag.
4. Seal and cook for 2 hours 30 minutes.
5. Preheat a frying pan to medium high heat.
6. Remove duck and fry the duck breast, skin side down, for 30 seconds.
7. Remove duck breast from pan serve with your favorite sides.

Nutrition

Calories: 106 Sodium: 117 mg, Dietary Fiber: 0g, Fat: 3.2g, Carbs: 0.7g, Protein: 17.7g

Aromatic
Lemon Thyme Chicken

Brighten up weeknight meals with succulent chicken seasoned with citrus and aromatic thyme.

Servings: 2
Prep time: 30 minutes
Cook time: 2 hours

2 boneless, skinless chicken breasts
6 sprigs thyme
2 garlic cloves, minced
Sea salt, to taste
White pepper, to taste
1 lemon, thinly sliced
1½ tablespoons olive oil

1. Add all ingredients to a resealable bag except olive oil and marinate for 30 minutes.
2. Pre-heat the water bath to 141°F.
3. Add chicken to sous vide water bath and cook for 2 hours.
4. Heat olive oil in a frying pan on medium-high.
5. Remove chicken from water bath and sear on both sides for 2 minutes.
6. Serve and enjoy!

Nutrition
Calories: 643 Sodium: 248 mg, Dietary Fiber: 3.9g, Fat: 50g, Carbs: 8.9g, Protein: 43.5g

Rich and Tasty
Duck à l'Orange

A 1960s delicacy, inspired by famous chef Julia Child - this recipe is full of flavor to compliment duck's rich taste and texture.

Servings: 2 - 4
Prep time: 20 minutes
Cook time: 2 hrs 30 minutes

2 small duck breasts
1 orange, sliced
4 garlic cloves, smashed
1 shallot, smashed
4 thyme sprigs
1/2 tablespoon black peppercorns
1 tablespoon sherry vinegar
¼ cup red wine, like Merlot
2 tablespoons butter
Sea salt, to taste

1. Preheat a sous vide cooker water bath to 135°F.
2. Add the duck breasts with slices of orange, garlic, shallots, thyme and peppercorns to a vacuum bag.
3. Seal and cook for 2 hours 30 minutes.
4. Preheat a frying pan to medium high heat.
5. Remove duck from bag and set bag aside.
6. Fry the duck breast, skin side down, for 30 seconds.
7. Remove duck breast from pan and keep warm.
8. Add vinegar and red wine to frying pan to deglaze leftover fat.
9. Add the contents of the vacuum bag and cook for about 6 minutes over medium heat.
10. Fold in the butter and season with salt and pepper.
11. Slice the duck breast into 2 inch medallions, top with sauce, and serve.

Nutrition
Calories: 205 Sodium: 104 mg, Dietary Fiber: 2.4g, Fat: 9.3g, Carbs: 10g, Protein: 18.7g

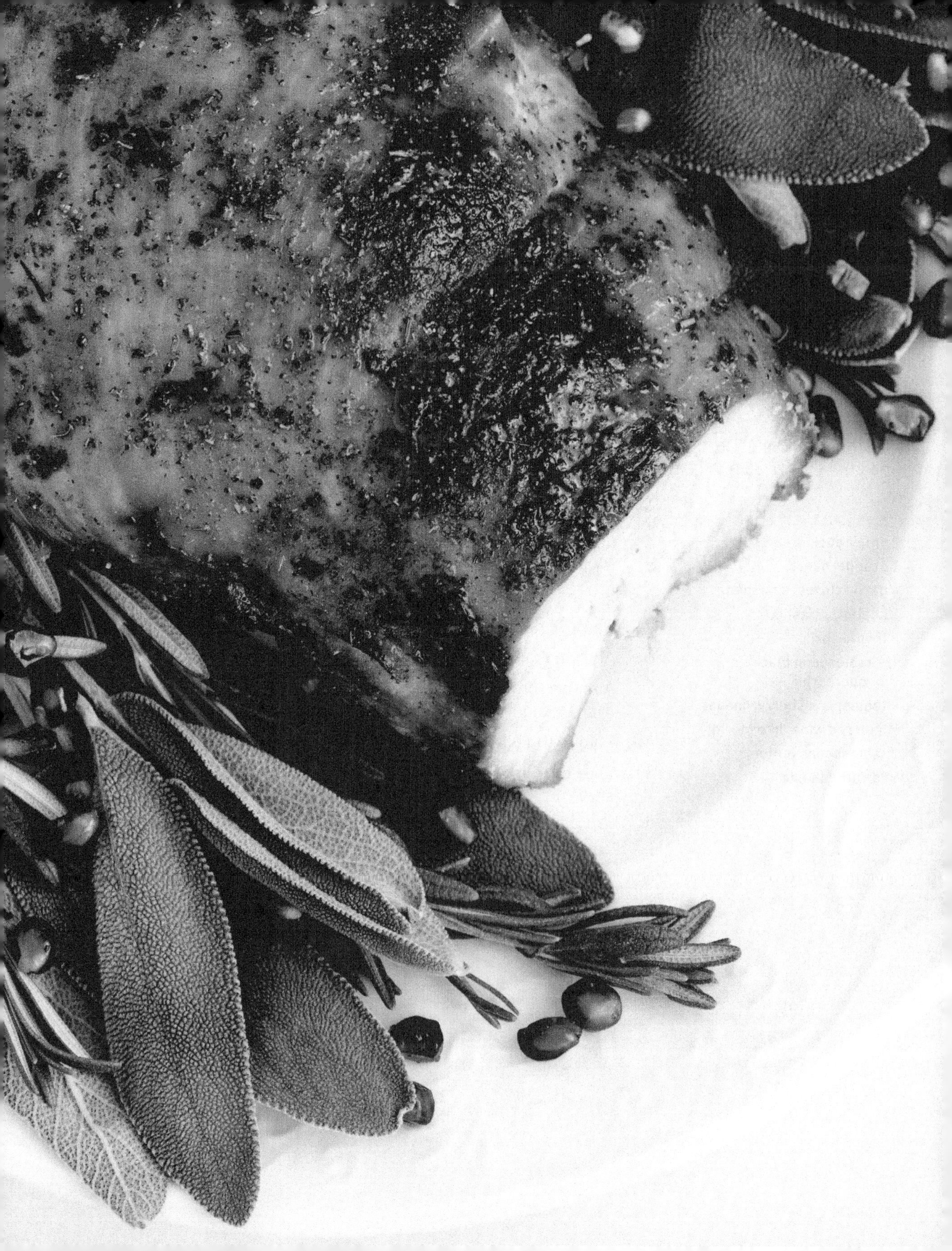

The Moist Delicious
Thanksgiving Turkey

Sous vide turkey is moist, delicious, and absolutely perfect for a "no fuss" Thanksgiving feast for the whole family.

Servings: 6
Prep time: 60 minutes
Cook time: 2 hrs 30 minutes
(4 to 6 hours for turkey legs)

14 pound turkey
Salt
1 stick unsalted butter
8 garlic cloves, minced
4 sprigs sage
4 sprigs thyme
4 sprigs rosemary

1. Defrost turkey according to the instructions on the packaging.
2. Preheat sous vide water bath 149°F.
3. Remove the packaged gizzards inside the turkey cavity.
4. Remove the thighs and drumsticks with a boning knife, then remove the wings of the turkey.
5. Cut out the rib cage, with kitchen shears, and save for stock or gravy.
6. Cut the breast in half, down the middle with boning knife, and keep the bone in.
7. Place the thighs and wings in one gallon vacuum bag and do not overlap.
8. Place drumsticks in another bag, turkey breast in a third and fourth bag.
9. Add 2 smashed cloves garlic, 1 sprig of each herb, and two tablespoons of butter to each bag.
10. Seal with a vacuum sealer or use the water displacement method.
11. Take care that the turkey pieces inside the bags are completely submerged during sous vide.
12. Cook for 2 hours 30 minutes; legs will be most tender when cooked at 4 to 6 hours.
13. Here, you can crisp in a cast iron skillet for 3 minutes on each side and serve immediately with your favorite trimmings.

Nutrition

Calories: 1960 Sodium: 880 mg, Dietary Fiber: 2.6g, Fat: 68.9g, Carbs: 5.4g, Protein: 310.9g

Spicy Honey Sriracha Wings

Sweet honey meets spicy sriracha for a batch of wings that will knock your socks off!

Servings: 4 - 6
Prep time: 5 minutes
Cook time: 45 minutes

1 lb. chicken wings
1/2 teaspoon sea salt
1/2 teaspoon paprika
1/2 teaspoon garlic
1/2 teaspoon ginger
1/2 teaspoon black pepper

For the glaze:
1 tablespoon sesame oil
2 tablespoons soy sauce
2 tablespoons honey
2 tablespoons Sriracha

1. Preheat sous vide water bath to 140°F.
2. Mix spices in a mixing bowl, and toss wings to coat.
3. Add wings to a vacuum bag.
4. Cook the wings for 40 minutes.
5. Combine glaze ingredients in a large mixing bowl.
6. Transfer chicken wings in an ice bath.
7. For crispy wings, fry in a Dutch oven on 375 °F for 1 to 2 minutes, or until golden.
8. Toss the wings in the glaze and serve hot!

Nutrition
Calories: 195 Sodium: 557 mg, Dietary Fiber: 0.2g, Fat: 9.3g, Carbs: 7.6g, Protein: 22.3g

Delicate Rosemary Chicken

Aromatic and delicious, this chicken is best paired with salad and roasted eggplant for a Mediterranean meal to die for!

Servings: 4
Prep time: 1 hour
Cook time: 2 hours

For the brine:

2 cups of chicken stock
4 tablespoons salt
2 tablespoons brown sugar

For the rosemary sauce:

1 stick of butter
2 teaspoons rosemary, chopped
1 teaspoon garlic powder
1/2 teaspoon paprika
1/2 teaspoon sea salt
1/2 teaspoon black pepper
1 tablespoon olive oil

1. Add chicken to a shallow dish with brine, cover, and refrigerate for 60 minutes.
2. Pre-heat the water bath to 141°F.
3. Combine rosemary sauce ingredients in a mixing bowl.
4. Add chicken breasts to a vacuum bag and seal.
5. Add to sous vide bath and cook for 2 hours.
6. Add rosemary sauce to a pan on medium-high heat and brown for 5 minutes.
7. Remove chicken from bags, coat with butter, and brown in a frying pan on medium-high, on both sides, for 2 minutes.
8. Serve and enjoy!

Nutrition

Calories: 195 Sodium: 557 mg, Dietary Fiber: 0.2g, Fat: 9.3g, Carbs: 7.6g, Protein: 22.3g

Flavorful Chicken Marsala

Italian wine adds depth and flavor to chicken in this yummy way to really make good use out of your Everie!

Servings: 4
Prep time: 15 minutes
Cook time: 3 hours

4 chicken breasts
2 sprigs fresh thyme
Sea salt
Black pepper

For the chicken marsala topping:

1 cup unbleached flour
Olive oil
3 cups sliced baby portabella mushrooms
3/4 cup Marsala wine
3/4 cup chicken stock
3 tablespoons butter
4 tablespoons chopped Italian parsley

1. Pre-heat the water bath to 141°F.
2. Lightly salt and pepper the chicken breasts and place in a vacuum bag with thyme and seal.
3. Add to water bath and cook for 2 hours.
4. Heat olive oil in a sauté pan over high heat.
5. Preheat oven to warm.
6. Remove the sous vide chicken breasts from the sous vide bath, pat dry with a paper towel, and dredge them in the flour.
7. Sear the chicken breasts for 1 minute per side.
8. Remove and place on a baking sheet in the warm oven.
9. Turn heat to medium high for the sauté pan and melt 1 tablespoon of butter.
10. Add mushrooms and cook until they brown and release their liquid; about 4 to 6 minutes.
11. Turn heat down to medium and add the Marsala wine to the pan; simmer for 1 minute, scraping the bottom of the pan to dislodge the browned bits.
12. Add the chicken stock and simmer for 10 minutes to reduce sauce.
13. Fold the remaining 2 tablespoons of butter into the sauce, and plate the seared chicken breasts.
14. Spoon the Marsala sauce evenly over the chicken breasts.
15. Garnish with Italian parsley and serve.

Nutrition

Calories: 550 Sodium: 454 mg, Dietary Fiber: 2.1g, Fat: 23.6g, Carbs: 27.8g, Protein: 46.6g

Tempting
Teriyaki Chicken

Sweet and savory teriyaki chicken is delicious when served with your favorite Asian-style veggies sous vide on top of a bed of brown rice.

Servings: 1
Prep time: 5 minutes
Cook time: 2 hours

- 1 skinless, boneless chicken breast
- 1/2 teaspoon ginger juice
- 2 tablespoons sugar, plus 1 teaspoon
- 1/2 teaspoon salt
- 2 tablespoons soy sauce
- 2 tablespoons sake or mirin

1. Dry the chicken with a paper towel and then coat with the ginger juice.
2. Mix 1 teaspoon sugar and salt in a small bowl, and sprinkle on both sides of the chicken.
3. Add the chicken to a vacuum bag and seal; set aside to marinate for 30 minutes or overnight.
4. Preheat sous vide water bath to 140°F.
5. Add chicken and cook sous vide for 1 hour 30 minutes.
6. Combine the remaining sugar, soy sauce and sake in a small saucepan, bring to a boil, and cook until the sauce is thick, forming large shiny bubbles.
7. Remove sauce and place on warm until chicken is done.
8. Plate chicken, top with teriyaki sauce, and serve!

Nutrition

Calories: 300 Sodium: 3267 mg, Dietary Fiber: 0.4g, Fat: 4.1g, Carbs: 41.1g, Protein: 27.1g

Tender Turkey Breast

Juicy turkey breast cooks up in no time when you sous vide it in your Everie with this delicious recipe.

Servings: 6
Prep time: 15 minutes
Cook time: 2 hrs 30 minutes

- 2 lb. turkey breast, cut into 4 pieces
- 1 tablespoon olive oil
- 4 sprigs fresh thyme
- 1 cup chicken stock, divided in 4
- Celery salt
- Black pepper

1. Preheat sous vide bath to 145°F.
2. Place turkey breasts on a flat surface and rub each piece with olive oil, celery salt, and pepper.
3. Place seasoned turkey breasts into their own Ziploc bags, add a sprig of thyme to each, ¼ cup stock, and vacuum seal.
4. Fully submerge bags and cook for 2 hours 30 minutes.
5. Remove cooked turkey breasts from bag and pat dry with a paper towel.
6. To crisp the breasts, sear in a cast iron skillet on each side for 3 minutes.
7. Serve immediately with your favorite sides.

Nutrition

Calories: 188 Sodium: 1745 mg, Dietary Fiber: 1.8g, Fat: 5.1g, Carbs: 8.7g, Protein: 26.3g

Sous Vide Chicken Breast with Creamy Mushroom Sauce

Creamy mushroom sauce turns chicken into one delicious dish of earthy flavor when you use your Everie.

Servings: 2
Prep time: 25 minutes
Cook time: 1 hour 35 minutes

2 boneless, skinless chicken breasts
1/8 teaspoon sea salt

For the mushroom cream sauce:

3 shallots, finely chopped
2 large cloves garlic, minced
1 teaspoon olive oil
2 tablespoons butter
1 cup button mushrooms, sliced
2 tablespoons port wine
1/2 cup chicken stock
1 cup heavy cream
¼ teaspoon fresh ground black pepper

1. Preheat sous vide water bath to 140°F.
2. Salt chicken breasts evenly, place in vacuum bag, and seal.
3. Cook for 1 hour 30 minutes.
4. Add the olive oil to a frying pan on medium heat.
5. Add shallots and cook for 3 minutes.
6. Add the butter and garlic, and stir for 1 minute.
7. Turn stove up to medium-high, and add the mushrooms; cook until they release liquid and it evaporates.
8. Add the port wine and cook until it's nearly evaporated.
9. Add the stock and cook for 2 minutes, then fold in the cream until well-incorporated.
10. Cook over medium heat until the sauce thickens and finish with pepper.
11. Remove chicken from sous vide bath and plate.
12. Top with mushroom sauce and enjoy!

Nutrition

Calories: 653 Sodium: 692 mg, Dietary Fiber: 0.6g, Fat: 47.2g, Carbs: 9.1g, Protein: 45.9g

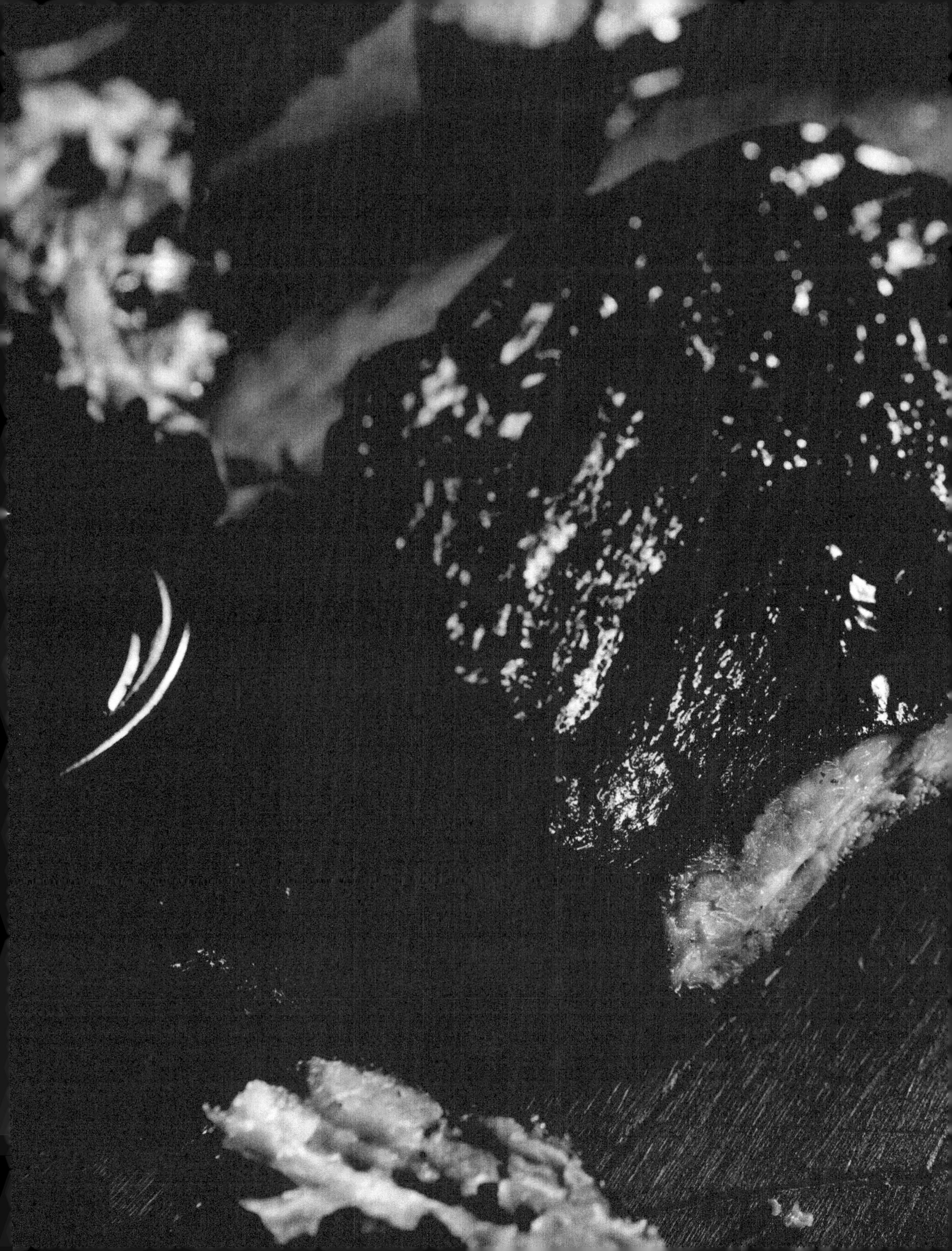

CHAPTER 7

Main Dishes
Pork

Melt-In-Your Mouth
Carnitas for Tacos

Carnitas are a melt in your mouth, juicy taco stuffing that is sure to please the whole family on Taco Night!

Servings: 8
Prep time: 5 minutes
Cook time: 12 to 20 hours

- 2 lbs. pork shoulder meat, removed from the bone
- 1 tablespoon brown sugar
- 1 teaspoon anise seed
- 1 teaspoon garlic powder
- 2 teaspoons kosher salt
- 1 teaspoon cinnamon
- 1 teaspoon lemon peel
- 2 slices of bacon
- Corn tortillas, for serving
- Salsa, for serving
- Sliced avocado, for serving

1. Preheat sous vide water bath to 165°F.
2. Add all ingredients to a large Ziploc bag.
3. With the top of the Ziploc bag open, carefully submerge the bag into the bottom of the water bath, without allowing any water into the bag itself.
4. Carefully seal the bag.
5. Cook for 12 to 20 hours.
6. Transfer pork from bag to a plate and pull apart with two forks.
7. Serve on tortillas with your favorite salsa and avocado.

Nutrition
Calories: 422 Sodium: 778 mg, Dietary Fiber: 2.1g, Fat: 31.3g, Carbs: 5.4g, Protein: 29g

Sous Vide
Beer Brined Pork Shoulder

Beer makes the perfect brine when it comes to cooking up a delicious pork shoulder for a party or tailgate.

Servings: 8
Prep time: 5 minutes
Cook time: 12 to 20 hours

- 2 lbs. pork shoulder meat, removed from the bone
- 6 cups craft beer, like Brooklyn Lager
- 1 teaspoon brining salt

1. Preheat sous vide water bath to 165°F.
2. Add all ingredients to a large Ziploc bag.
3. With the top of the Ziploc bag open, carefully submerge the bag into the bottom of the water bath, without allowing any water into the bag itself.
4. Carefully seal the bag.
5. Cook for 12 to 20 hours.
6. Transfer pork from bag to a plate and pull apart with forks or slice for sandwich meat.

Nutrition
Calories: 341 Sodium: 138 mg, Dietary Fiber: 0g, Fat: 24.3g, Carbs: 0.9g, Protein: 26.5g

Pork Tenderloin
with Cherry Salsa

Tender juicy pork is cooked to perfection when you sous vide this scrumptious cut of meat for the whole family.

Servings: 6 - 8
Prep time: 10 minutes
Cook time: 4 hrs 30 minutes

1 lb. pork tenderloin, trimmed and clean of silver skin
3 sprigs thyme
1 teaspoon garlic powder
½ teaspoon salt
½ teaspoon white pepper
2 tablespoons butter

For the cherry salsa:
3 cups cherries, pitted and roughly chopped
1/2 cup red onion
2 tablespoons lemon juice
1 tablespoon balsamic vinegar
1 teaspoon honey

1. Preheat sous vide water bath to 145°F.
2. Place pork loin and seasoning in a vacuum bag and seal airtight.
3. Cook for 4 hours 30 minutes.
4. Prepare cherry salsa: add all ingredients to a food processor and process to desired consistency.
5. Remove pork loin from sous vide bath, slice pork loin into 1 inch thick medallions, and serve topped with a dollop of salsa.

Nutrition
Calories: 150 Sodium: 207 mg, Dietary Fiber: 0.8g, Fat: 5g, Carbs: 10.3g, Protein: 15.2g

Lemongrass and Garlic
Roast Pork Belly Roll

Light, aromatic lemongrass elevates salty pork belly to a whole new level in this delicious flavor combination that will fast become a sous vide favorite.

Servings: 6
Prep time: 10 minutes
Cook time: 8 hours

1 lb. pork belly, leave whole
3 1/2 teaspoons sea salt
1/2 teaspoon pepper
1/4 cup olive oil
4 stalks lemongrass, white part only
1 whole garlic bulb, peeled
2 bell peppers, sliced into strips
Cooking string or Activa, to secure belly closed

1. Preheat sous vide water bath to 165°F.
2. Generously season pork belly with salt all over.
3. Lay skin side down.
4. Add lemongrass, bell pepper, and garlic, in a line in the belly's center, and drizzle with a little olive oil.
5. Roll belly into a log and tie with cooking string or secure shut with Activa.
6. Add pork belly to a large Ziploc bag.
7. With the top of the Ziploc bag open, carefully submerge the bag into the bottom of the water bath, without allowing any water into the bag itself.
8. Carefully seal the bag.
9. Cook for 8 hours.
10. Slice into 1 inch thick medallions and serve warm with your favorite sides.

Nutrition
Calories: 439 Sodium: 2315 mg, Dietary Fiber: 0.6g, Fat: 28.9g, Carbs: 4.4g, Protein: 35.5g

Juicy and Tender Pork Belly

Pork belly is a yummy way to whip up a cut of meat that you can serve with all of your favorite side dishes for an alternative family meal on the weekends.

Servings: 6 - 8
Prep time: 10 minutes
Cook time: 8 hours

2 pounds skinless, boneless pork belly
6 scallions, cut into 1-inch pieces
¼ cup honey
¼ cup soy sauce
3 tablespoons sambal oelek
1 tablespoon grapeseed oil

1. Preheat sous vide water bath to 165°F.
2. Add all ingredients to a large Ziploc bag.
3. With the top of the Ziploc bag open, carefully submerge the bag into the bottom of the water bath, without allowing any water into the bag itself.
4. Carefully seal the bag.
5. Cook for 8 hours.
6. Serve warm with your favorite sides.

Nutrition

Calories: 194 Sodium: 539 mg, Dietary Fiber: 0.4g, Fat: 5.2g, Carbs: 10.5g, Protein: 26.1g

Simply Delicious
Pork Chops

Sous vide pork chops are just the way to really put your Everie to good use when it comes to exploring new sous vide recipes.

Servings: 2
Prep time: 5 minutes
Cook time: 4 hours

2 bone in pork chops
Sea salt, to taste
Black pepper, to taste
1 teaspoon olive oil

1. Preheat a sous vide to 140°F.
2. Salt and pepper pork chops evenly on both sides.
3. Add pork to a large Ziploc bag and seal airtight.
4. Add pork chops to sous vide bath and cook for 4 hours.
5. Transfer pork to plate.
6. Heat olive oil in a frying pan, on medium high heat. Sear the pork chops for 1 minute per side and serve immediately.

Nutrition
Calories: 260 Sodium: 827 mg, Dietary Fiber: 0g, Fat: 14.3g, Carbs: 1g, Protein: 29g

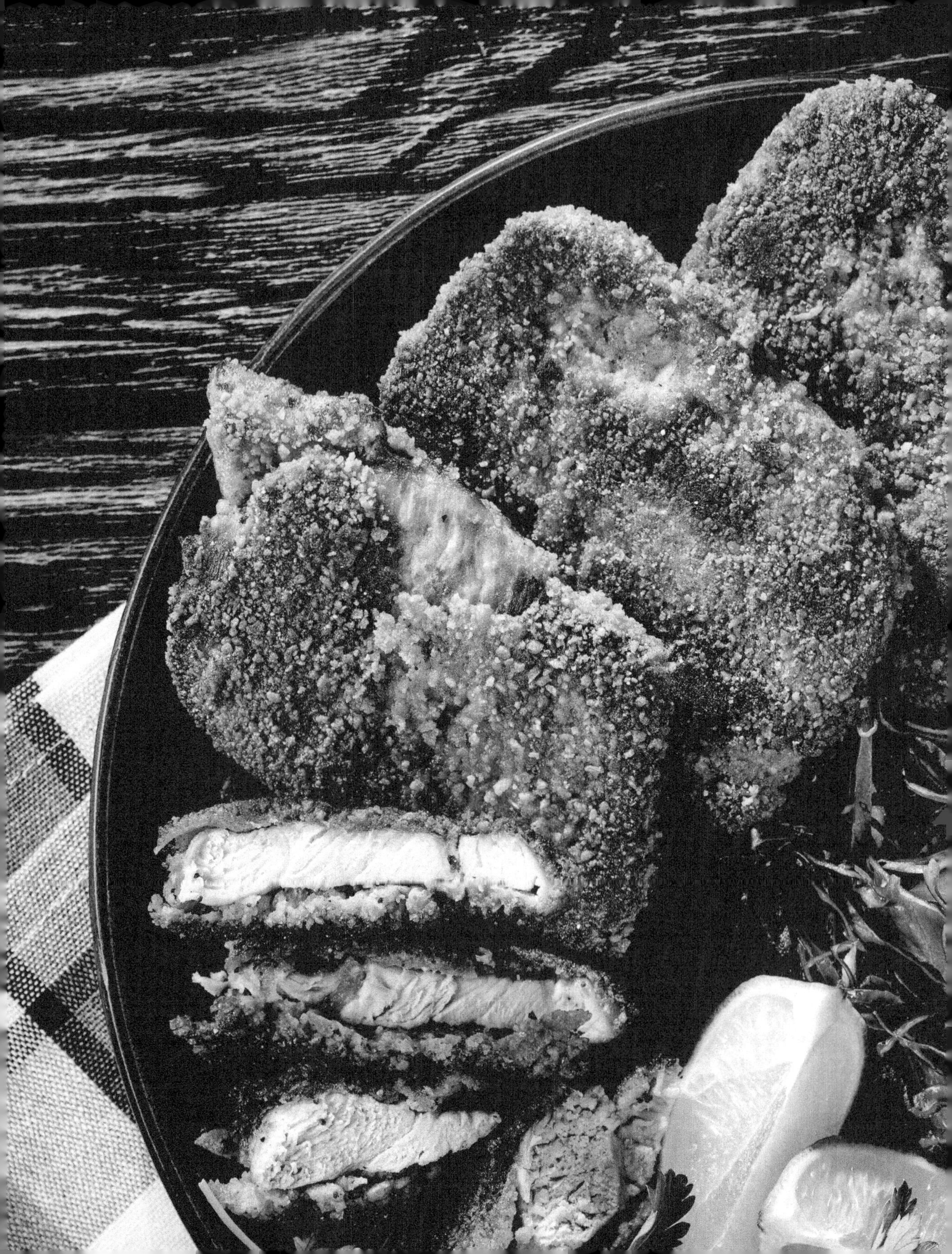

Lemony Herb Crusted
Pork Chops

Herb crusted pork chops topped with creamy, light Meyer lemon sauce really takes this delicious cut of meat to a whole new level.

Servings: 4
Prep time: 5 minutes
Cook time: 4 hours 5 minutes

4 bone-in pork chops
3 eggs, beaten
1 teaspoon whole milk

For the crust:

1 1/2 cups all-purpose flour
1 1/2 cups panko
2 tablespoons fresh basil, finely chopped
1 tablespoon fresh oregano, finely chopped
1/4 cup Parmesan, finely grated

1. Preheat a sous vide water bath to 140°F.
2. Add pork chops to vacuum bag, seal and cook for 4 hours.
3. Remove pork chops.
4. Whisk milk and egg together to make an egg wash.
5. Combine herb crust ingredients together in a large mixing bowl.
6. Dip a pork chop into the egg wash and fully coat.
7. Dip in the herb crust to coat evenly and transfer to a greased baking sheet; repeat until all pork chops are coated.
8. Broil for 2 - 3 minutes on each side until golden brown.
9. Transfer to plates and top with salt and pepper to serve.

Nutrition

Calories: 508 Sodium: 716 mg, Dietary Fiber: 3.6g, Fat: 12.4g, Carbs: 66.6g, Protein: 29.7g

Yummy Pulled Pork
with Chili Pepper BBQ Sauce

Be sure to grab buns and coleslaw to put together some yummy sandwiches all your friends and family will love with this recipe.

Servings: 8
Prep time: 5 minutes
Cook time: 12 - 20 hours

2 lbs. pork shoulder meat, removed from the bone
1 tablespoon brown sugar
1 teaspoon chili powder
1 teaspoon garlic powder
2 teaspoons kosher salt
1 teaspoon hot red pepper flakes
BBQ sauce, for serving

1. Preheat sous vide water bath to 165°F.
2. Add all ingredients, except sauce, to a large Ziploc bag.
3. With the top of the Ziploc bag open, carefully submerge the bag into the bottom of the water bath, without allowing any water into the bag itself and seal the bag.
4. Cook for 12 to 20 hours.
5. Transfer pork from bag to a plate and pull apart with two forks.
6. Add pork to a large mixing bowl and fold in BBQ sauce until well-covered.
7. Serve with bread to make sandwiches or with your favorite sides as the main dish.

Nutrition
Calories: 344 Sodium: 706 mg, Dietary Fiber: 0.2g, Fat: 24.4g, Carbs: 3.1g, Protein: 26.5g

Mouth-Water Bacon-Wrapped Pork Tenderloin

Crispy bacon wrapped pork tenderloin is super juicy and yummy when served with your favorite vegetables or salads for one delicious lunch or dinner option.

Servings: 6 - 8
Prep time: 10 minutes
Cook time: 5 hours

5 lb. pork loin
12 strips of bacon
2 teaspoons Activa, like Moo Glue
Parchment paper

1. Preheat sous vide water bath to 145°F.
2. Lay bacon strips on parchment paper as close as possible without overlapping.
3. Trim pork of all excess fat and sprinkle evenly all over with Activa (this will hold your bacon in place in lieu of tying it together).
4. Lay pork loin on top of the bacon.
5. Wrap bacon around the pork loin, securing ends, in a straight line all the way around the pork loin.
6. Place pork loin in a vacuum bag and seal airtight.
7. Cook for 4 1/2 hours.
8. Preheat oven to 350°F.
9. Remove pork tenderloin from bag and place on an elevated baking rack.
10. Roast for 20 to 30 minutes until bacon is crispy; check every 10 minutes as to not burn the bacon.
11. Slice into 1 inch thick medallions and serve.

Nutrition

Calories: 836 Sodium: 626 mg, Dietary Fiber: 0g, Fat: 53g, Carbs: 0g, Protein: 83.5g

Beer-Infused Sausages

Spice-filled sausages are yummy when you sous vide and assemble into sandwiches or even serve as a delicious brunch day treat with eggs and pancakes.

Servings: 6 - 8
Prep time: 20 minutes
Cook time: 4 hours

3 lbs. natural-casing raw bratwurst sausage links
6 ounces beer, like Coors Light
Buns and condiments, for serving

1. Preheat a sous vide water bath to 160°F.
2. Add sausages to a vacuum bag in a single layer.
3. Add 5 tablespoons beer to each bag.
4. Seal the bags, but not airtight, so the sausages are not squeezed.
5. Add sausages to water bath and cook for 4 hours.
6. Remove sausages from bags and discard beer.
7. Dry sausages carefully on a paper towel–lined plate.
8. Here, you can grill for 3 minutes each to sear or serve immediately on buns with your favorite toppings.

Nutrition

Calories: 125 Sodium: 288 mg, Dietary Fiber: 0.1g, Fat: 9.5g, Carbs: 3.4g, Protein: 4.8g

Oh-So-Tender
Baby Back Ribs

Tender Baby Back Ribs are gonna fall right off the bone when you prepare them using your Everie sous vide!

Servings: 3
Prep time: 10 minutes
Cook time: 9 hours

1 rack of baby-back pork ribs, cut into 3 pieces
2 bottles hickory smoked BBQ sauce, like Kraft
2 tablespoons BBQ poultry rub, like Lawry's

1. Preheat the sous vide water bath to 165°F.
2. Mix the spice rub seasoning together in a mixing bowl until combined well.
3. Rub the ribs evenly and generously with the spice mixture.
4. Add the racks to individual small vacuum bags and seal.
5. Submerge in the water bath and cook for 9 hours.
6. Preheat a greased grill or grill pan to high heat.
7. Remove the racks from the bath.
8. Brush each rack evenly with barbecue sauce.
9. Sear ribs for 30 seconds per side to caramelize the sauce, serve immediately with your favorite sides.

Nutrition
Calories: 637 Sodium: 1767 mg, Dietary Fiber: 3g, Fat: 31.3g, Carbs: 59g, Protein: 30g

Kung Pao Short Ribs

Spicy stick to your ribs recipes are also a great way to put your Everie to good use!

Servings: 2 - 4
Prep time: 10 minutes
Cook time: 4 hrs 10 minutes

4 (8 ounce) boneless beef short ribs
½ teaspoon salt
½ teaspoon black pepper

For the Korean BBQ Sauce:

1 ½ cups brown sugar
1 ½ cups soy sauce
½ cup mirin
½ cup water
2 tablespoons rice wine vinegar
3 tablespoons chili paste
1 tablespoon sesame oil
1 teaspoon ground black pepper
1 tablespoon fresh ginger, grated
6 garlic cloves, crushed
1 green onion, finely chopped
2 tablespoons cornstarch
2 tablespoons water

1. Preheat a sous vide bath to 130°F.
2. Combine the BBQ sauce ingredients, in a large saucepan, and bring to a boil on high heat; cook for 7 minutes.
3. Combine the cornstarch and water in a small mixing bowl until well-combined.
4. Fold the cornstarch mixture into the boiling sauce.
5. Whisk to combine well, reduce heat to medium and cook 3 minutes.
6. Turn the heat off and set aside the sauce.
7. Salt and pepper the short ribs evenly.
8. Add the short ribs and 1/3 cup of the BBQ sauce to a large vacuum bag and seal.
9. Submerge in the water bath and cook for 4 hours.
10. Preheat a greased grill or grill pan to high heat.
11. Remove the short ribs from the bath.
12. Brush again, all over, with barbecue sauce.
13. Sear ribs for 30 seconds per side to create sticky, delicious glazed ribs!

Nutrition

Calories: 831 Sodium: 6243 mg, Dietary Fiber: 1.2g, Fat: 19.6g, Carbs: 85.7g, Protein: 76.2g

Scrumptious
BBQ Ribs

Mouthwatering ribs are just the way to anyone's heart when you follow this scrumptious recipe using your sous vide!

Servings: 2
Prep time: 10 minutes
Cook time: 12 - 24 hours

2 racks of baby-back pork ribs
2 bottles of your favorite BBQ sauce

For the rub:
2 tablespoons garlic powder
2 tablespoons onion powder
2 tablespoons chili powder
2 tablespoons smoked paprika
2 tablespoons sea salt
2 tablespoons black pepper

1. Preheat the sous vide water bath to 150°F.
2. Mix the spice rub seasoning together in a mixing bowl until combined well.
3. Rub the ribs evenly and generously with the spice mixture.
4. Brush each side of the ribs with barbecue sauce.
5. Add the racks into a large vacuum bag and seal.
6. Submerge in the water bath and cook for 12 to 24 hours.
7. Preheat a greased grill or grill pan to high heat.
8. Remove the racks from the bath.
9. Brush again, all over, with barbecue sauce.
10. Sear ribs for 30 seconds to 1 minute per side to caramelize the sauce and add a savory flavor.
11.

Nutrition
Calories: 1055 Sodium: 8589 mg, Dietary Fiber: 9.6g, Fat: 51.3g, Carbs: 114.4g, Protein: 36.6g

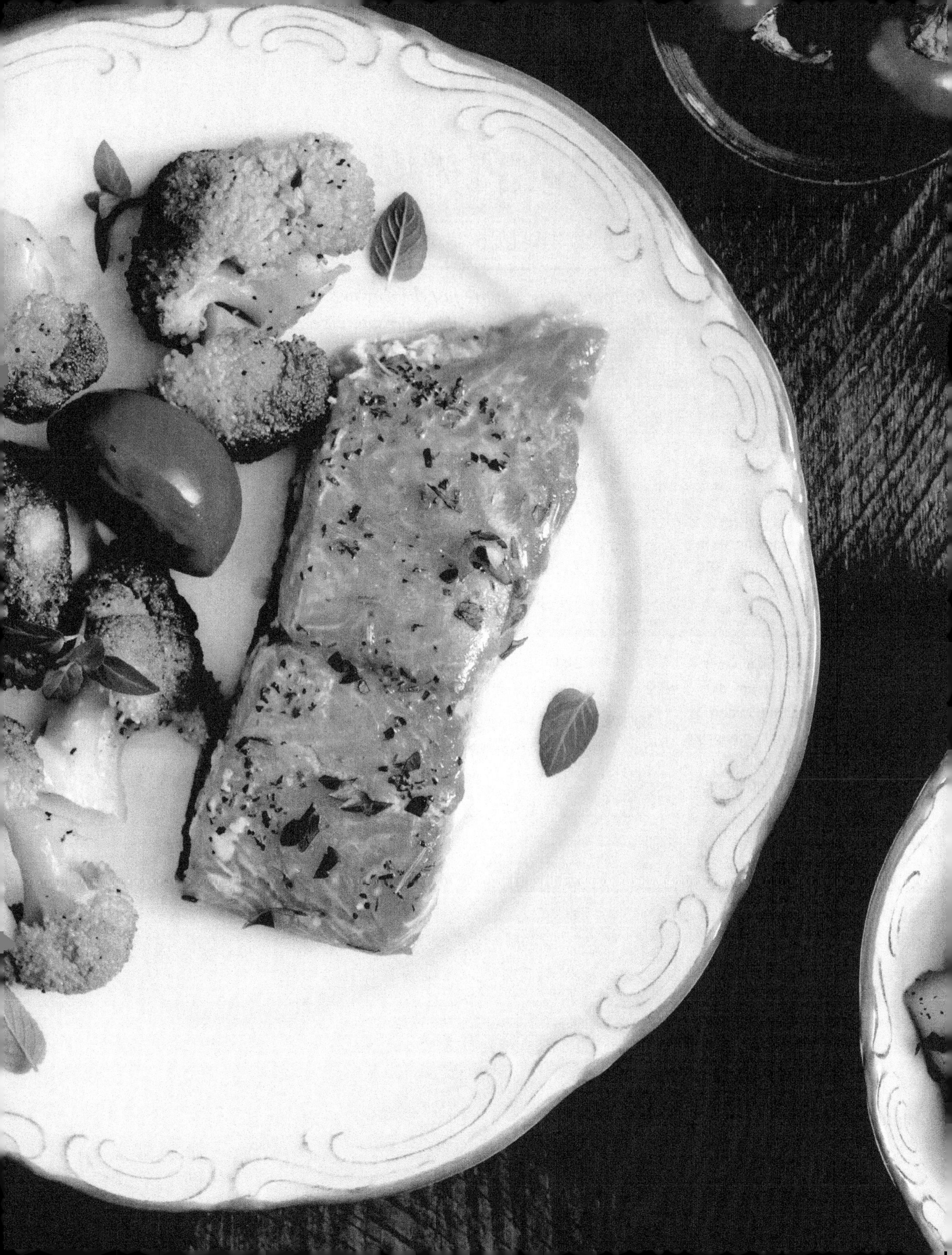

CHAPTER

8

Main Dishes

Seafood

Sous Vide
Cajun Tilapia

Whip up some good ol' "country food" when you perfectly season sous vide Tilapia with delicious Cajun seasoning.

Servings: 2
Prep time: 10 minutes
Cook time: 30 minutes

1 lb. skinless tilapia fillets
¼ cup Cajun seasoning
Olive oil, for garnish

1. Preheat a sous vide water bath to 134°F.
2. Rinse and pat the tilapia dry with paper towels.
3. Coat each fillet evenly with Cajun seasoning and place in a large vacuum seal bag.
4. Seal and cook for 30 minutes.
5. Transfer to plates and top with a drizzle of olive oil to serve.

Nutrition
Calories: 700 Sodium: 600 mg, Dietary Fiber: 0g, Fat: 7.9g, Carbs: 0g, Protein: 157.9g

Low-Tech High-Taste
Salmon with Herb Butter

Whip up salmon in a jiffy when you use the low-tech version of cooking salmon layered with luxurious herb butter.

Servings: 2
Prep time: 10 minutes
Cook time: 35 minutes

2 large salmon fillets

For the butter:
½ cup unsalted butter
1 teaspoon herbs de Provence
pinch of sea salt

1. Preheat a sous vide water bath to 125°F.
2. Place salmon in vacuum bags and seal airtight.
3. Cook 30 minutes.
4. Add the sauce ingredients to a small saucepan and heat on medium for five minutes; reduce to a low keep warm until salmon is done.
5. Remove salmon, plate, top with butter sauce, and serve!

Nutrition
Calories: 642 Sodium: 522 mg, Dietary Fiber: 0g, Fat: 57g, Carbs: 0g, Protein: 35g

Delightful Crispy Skin Salmon

Bring a delightful dimension to your delicate salmon with crispy skin that makes for one healthy way to enjoy Omega-3 packed meals.

Servings: 2
Prep time: 10 minutes
Cook time: 35 minutes

2 large salmon fillets
1 teaspoon sea salt
1 tablespoon honey
1/2 cup vegetable stock
2 cups ice water

1. Preheat a sous vide water bath to 125°F.
2. Place salmon, sea salt, honey and stock in vacuum bags and seal leaving some room for the brine to move.
3. Cook 30 minutes.
4. Preheat a frying pan to high and grease with non-stick cooking spray.
5. Remove salmon and submerge in an ice bath to halt cooking.
6. Sear salmon skin down for 5 minutes until crispy.
7. Plate and serve!

Nutrition
Calories: 269 Sodium: 1035 mg, Dietary Fiber: 0.2g, Fat: 11g, Carbs: 8.9g, Protein: 34.7g

Coconut Party
Shrimp

Sweet meets salty in this gorgeous recipe that you can use as a main dish with sides or serve with a sweet chili sauce as an appetizer or party food.

Servings: 4 - 8
Prep time: 5 minutes
Cook time: 15 minutes

1 lb. large shrimp
1 lime, juiced
1 can coconut milk
1 teaspoon Thai curry paste
1/2 teaspoon fresh ginger

1. Preheat your water bath to 131°F.
2. Add ingredients to a resealable plastic bag and toss shrimp to coat, seal, and place in the water bath.
3. Cook 15 minutes
4. Remove the shrimp to a bowl and serve warm.

Nutrition
Calories: 162 Sodium: 169 mg, Dietary Fiber: 1.4g, Fat: 9.1g, Carbs: 9.8g, Protein: 12.3g

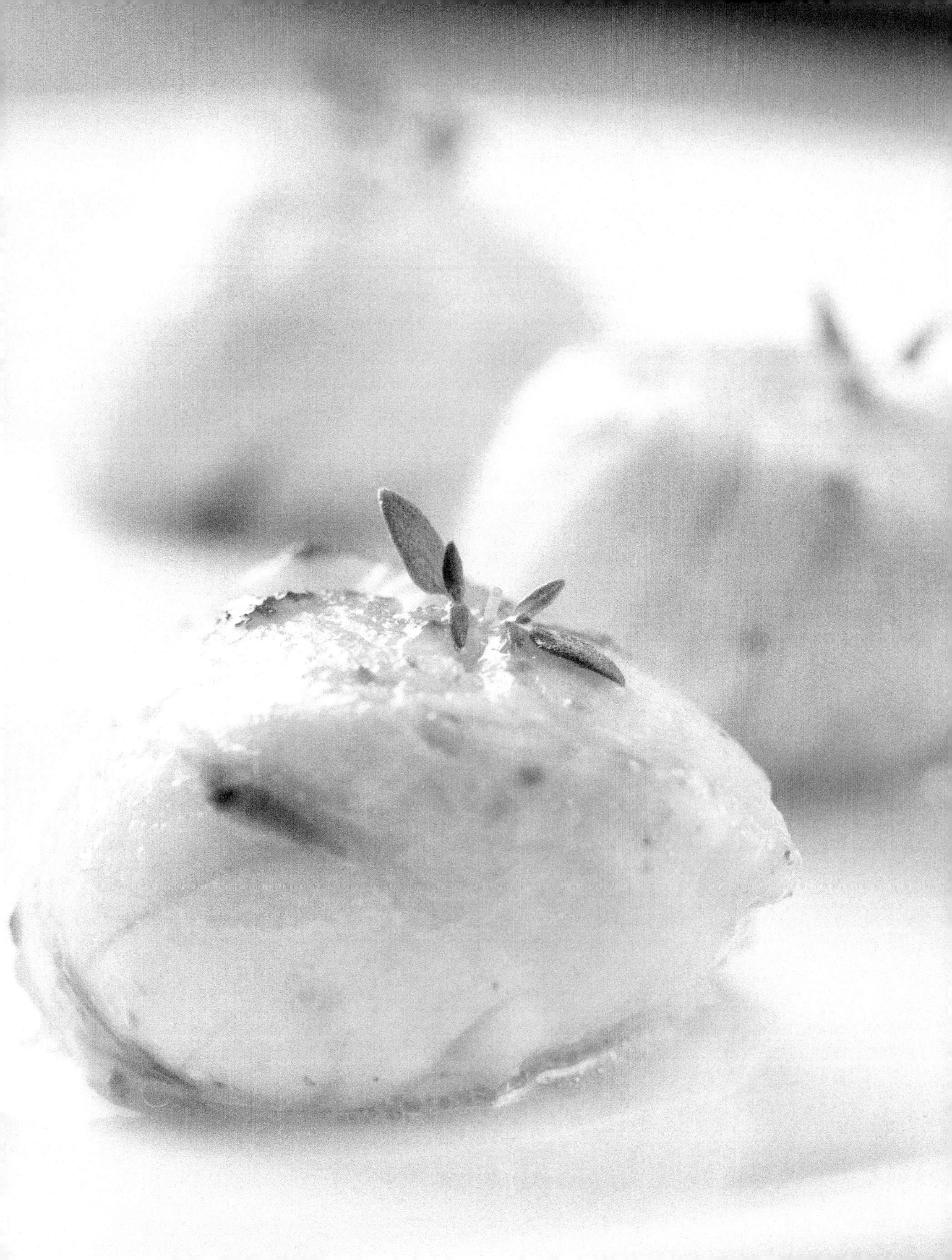

Richly Intense
Brown Butter Scallops

Turn ordinary scallops into a rich treat when you top them with a toasted brown butter for one amazingly intense dish!

Servings: 2
Prep time: 5 minutes
Cook time: 35 minutes

1 package scallops
2 teaspoons brown butter, divided

1. Preheat your sous vide bath to 140°F.
2. Pat your scallops dry with a paper towel.
3. Place scallops and 1 teaspoon brown butter in a vacuum bag.
4. Vacuum seal airtight.
5. Place the bag in the water and ensure that it stays submerged.
6. Cook for 40 minutes.
7. Heat remaining brown butter in a pan over high heat.
8. Add scallops to the pan and sear for 30 seconds per side until golden.
9. Serve topped with more brown butter or alongside your favorite veggies.

Nutrition
Calories: 71 Sodium: 96 mg, Dietary Fiber: 0g, Fat: 4.1g, Carbs: 1g, Protein: 7.2g

Paccheri Pasta
with Clams

A beautiful pasta from Campania, paccheri is elevated to be one very special dish with the light salty flavor of clams.

Servings: 2 - 4
Prep time: 15 minutes
Cook time: 1 hour 10 minutes

- 1 package paccheri pasta
- 1 lb. Clams, shelled
- 1 punnet cherry tomatoes
- ¼ cup sweet onion, like Vandalia, chopped
- 1 pinch red chili flakes, plus more for garnish
- Fine sea salt, to taste
- Fresh ground black pepper, to taste
- 2 tablespoons flat-leaf parsley, chopped
- Olive oil, plus more for garnish
- 1 garlic clove, smashed
- ½ teaspoon lemon zest, divided for garnish

1. Preheat sous vide water bath to 149°F.
2. Rinse clams and place them in a vacuum bag with a little olive oil, the chilli pepper and 1 garlic clove; immerse in the sous vide for 1 hour.
3. Cook the paccheri according to the package directions.
4. Sauté tomatoes and onions in a frying pan on medium-high heat until tomatoes burst, about 5 to 10 minutes.
5. Remove clams from sous vide.
6. Add pasta, clams, and tomato mix to a large mixing bowl and toss to coat.
7. Evenly distribute to plates and garnish with a heavy drizzle of olive oil and pinch of parsley, chili flakes, and lemon zest.

Nutrition

Calories: 246 Sodium: 488 mg, Dietary Fiber: 0.8g, Fat: 1.9g, Carbs: 48.9g, Protein: 8.2g

Delicious Dungeness Crab

King of the sea, the heart shaped Dungeness crab will warm your food loving heart when prepared sous vide.

Servings: 2
Prep time: 15 minutes
Cook time: 46 minutes

1 Dungeness crab
Clarified butter, for serving

1. Preheat sous vide water bath to 154°F.
2. Bring a large pot of water to a rolling boil on high heat.
3. Fully submerge the Dungeness crab in the boiling water for 1 minute to blanch.
4. Transfer the crab to a vacuum bag and seal airtight.
5. Cook for 45 minutes.
6. Remove, place on a serving platter, and serve with clarified butter.

Nutrition

Calories: 94 Sodium: 148 mg, Dietary Fiber: 0g, Fat: 6.3g, Carbs: 0g, Protein: 8.8g

Easy Lobster Tails

You can even whip up the most perfectly delicate lobster tails when you use your Everie.

Servings: 4
Prep time: 10 minutes
Cook time: 1 hour

4 lobster tails
1 tablespoon olive oil
½ cup sweet onion, sliced thin
1 celery stalk, sliced 1/8-inch thick
3 garlic cloves, smashed
2 tablespoons tomato paste
1 teaspoon white pepper

1. Preheat sous vide water bath to 131°F.
2. Place ingredients into a vacuum seal bag and seal. Place bag in sous vide.
3. Cook for 1 hour.
4. Remove from water bath, plate and serve with your favorite sous vide side dishes.

Nutrition

Calories: 177 Sodium: 717 mg, Dietary Fiber: 0.9g, Fat: 4.8g, Carbs: 4.1g, Protein: 28.3g

Luxurious Butter-Poached Lobster

Butter poached lobster is one of the most luxurious ways to serve up seafood in your sous vide.

Servings: 4
Prep time: 5 minutes
Cook time: 1 hour

2 lobster tails
10 tablespoons butter
Fresh parsley, chopped

1. Preheat sous vide water bath to 131°F.
2. Place ingredients into a vacuum seal bag and seal. Place bag in sous vide.
3. Cook for 1 hour.
4. Remove from water bath, plate and serve with your favorite sous vide side dishes.

Nutrition

Calories: 320 Sodium: 558 mg, Dietary Fiber: 0.1g, Fat: 29.4g, Carbs: 0.2g, Protein: 14.2g

Oysters
Sous Vide

Oyster lovers rejoice! This recipe will have you devouring your favorite treat sous vide style.

Servings: 4 - 8
Prep time: 3 minutes
Cook time: 5 minutes

25 Blue Point Oysters, raw and unshucked
Horseradish, for serving
Tabasco, for serving
Lemon wedges, for serving

1. Heat your water bath to 185°F.
2. Line vacuum bag with aluminum foil, so the oyster shell does not pierce the pouch.
3. Vacuum seal.
4. Cook for 5 minutes.
5. Remove oysters from the pouch and serve with horseradish, tabasco, and lemon wedges.

Nutrition
Calories: 47 Sodium: 45 mg, Dietary Fiber: 0.1g, Fat: 0.6g, Carbs: 1.9g, Protein: 35g

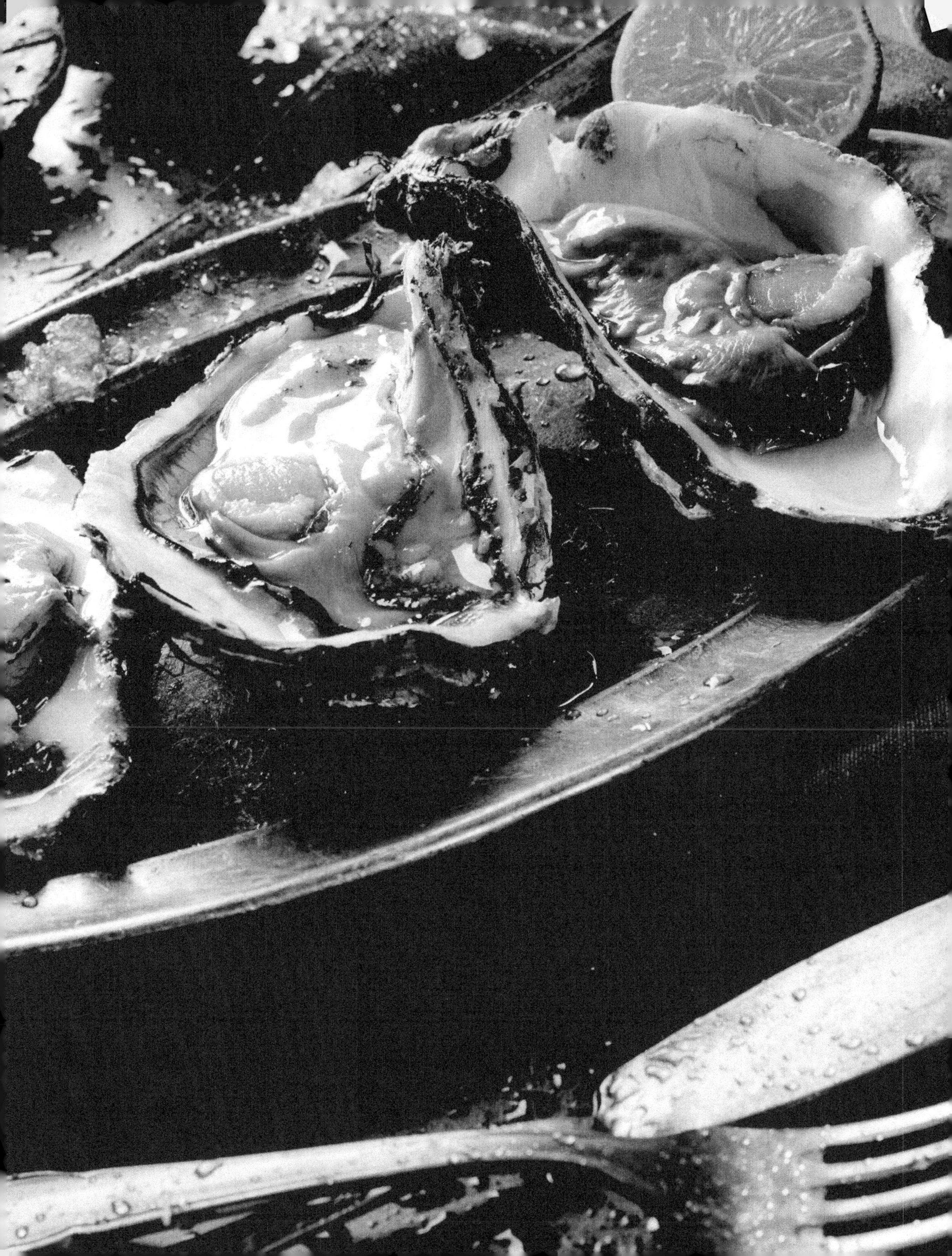

Light and Lemony
Octopus

Light and airy, octopus is a delicious way to serve up something special with your sous vide.

Servings: 4
Prep time: 5 minutes
Cook time: 4 hours

- 1 lb. octopus tentacles, cleaned and brined with salt
- 1/4 teaspoon ground black pepper
- 1 pinch sea salt, plus more for seasoning
- ½ teaspoon lemon juice
- ¼ teaspoon lemon zest
- Premium olive oil, like Partanna for garnish
- Lemon wedges, for garnish

1. Preheat the sous vide bath to 180°F.
2. Add the ingredients, except olive oil, to a vacuum bag, seal and place in bath.
3. Cook for around 4 hours.
4. Remove the octopus, and brush the tentacles with olive oil and lightly salt.
5. Prepare a skillet on high heat and sauté the octopus for 5 minutes, or until the edges are crispy.
6. Serve with lemon wedges to garnish.

Nutrition
Calories: 459 Sodium: 1077 mg, Dietary Fiber: 2g, Fat: 19.5g, Carbs: 34.1g, Protein: 32g

Mediterranean-Style Tilapia with Tomato, Olives and Oregano

A Mediterranean inspired dish, Tilapia is perfectly seasoned with oregano, olives and tomatoes for an out of this world combination.

Servings: 2
Prep time: 10 minutes
Cook time: 35 minutes

- 1 lb. skinless tilapia fillets
- 2 tablespoons tomato paste
- 1 lemon, juiced
- 1 tablespoon extra virgin olive oil, plus 1 teaspoon
- 1 clove garlic, minced
- 1 teaspoon dried oregano
- 1/4 teaspoon celery seed

For the topping:

- 2 tablespoons parmesan cheese
- 1 teaspoon olive oil
- Sliced lemon, for serving
- 8 black olives, pitted and roughly chopped, for serving
- Chopped fresh parsley, for serving

1. Preheat a sous vide water bath to 134°F.
2. Rinse and pat the fish dry with paper towels, and place in a large vacuum seal bag.
3. Mix lemon juice, tomato paste, 1 tablespoon olive oil, garlic, oregano, celery seed, and pinch of salt and black pepper in mixing bowl.
4. Add fish and toss to coat.
5. Add to vacuum bag, seal and cook for 30 minutes.
6. Preheat broiler to high when fish is 5 minutes from done.
7. Remove fish, place on greased baking sheet, top evenly with parmesan cheese and drizzle with remaining 1 tablespoon olive oil.
8. Broil fish for two minutes or until golden.
9. Transfer to plates and top with lemon slices, olives, and parsley to serve.

Nutrition

Calories: 949 Sodium: 996 mg, Dietary Fiber: 2.6g, Fat: 34g, Carbs: 9.2g, Protein: 160.5g

Lovely Lobster Pasta

Lobster pasta is a decadent way to use your sous vide and really treat your family to a lovely dinner.

Servings: 2 - 4
Prep time: 10 minutes
Cook time: 1 hour

4 frozen lobster tails, thawed and removed from shells
8 tablespoons unsalted butter
1 teaspoon garlic, minced and divided
2 sprigs parsley, chopped
1/4 teaspoon sea salt
3 tablespoons olive oil, divided
1 package pappardelle pasta

For the sauce:

4 cups heavy cream
1/3 cup sweet onion, chopped fine
¼ cup tomato paste
2 plum tomatoes, chopped
1/2 cup dry white wine
2 tablespoons white wine vinegar
1/4 teaspoon white pepper
1 teaspoon garlic powder
1 teaspoon garlic, minced and divided
4 large basil leaves, finely chopped for garnish

1. Preheat the water bath to 131°F.
2. Season the lobster with sea salt.
3. Place the lobster, butter, garlic, 1 teaspoon olive oil, and parsley into a vacuum bag, seal and place in bath.
4. Cook for 1 hour.
5. Heat remaining oil in a large saucepan over medium heat.
6. Add onion and sauté 5 minutes.
7. Add remaining garlic and sauté 3 minutes.
8. Fold in tomatoes, wine, vinegar, garlic powder, and pepper; simmer for 5 minutes.
9. Fold in the cream and bring to a boil, and reduce to medium-low.
10. Season with a pinch of sea salt and stir occasionally until sauce thickens, about 20 minutes.
11. Cook and drain the pasta per directions on the box.
12. Remove the lobster from the water bath and empty the vacuum sealer bag, saving only the lobster.
13. Cut the tails into 1 inch pieces and add to the sauce.
14. Plate the pasta, top with lobster and sauce, and a pinch of basil leaves.

Nutrition

Calories: 951 Sodium: 766 mg, Dietary Fiber: 2.8g, Fat: 79.4g, Carbs: 33.9g, Protein: 24.3g

Maple Bourbon Pecan Salmon

Smoky sweet salmon is the perfect way to serve up a healthy, delicious dinner in no time.

Servings: 2
Prep time: 10 minutes
Cook time: 35 minutes

2 large salmon fillets
1/2 cup pure maple syrup, like Vermont
1/4 cup bourbon, like Makers Mark
1/4 cup orange juice
1/2 teaspoon orange zest
1/4 cup pecans, chopped
pinch of sea salt

1. Preheat a sous vide water bath to 125°F.
2. Place salmon in vacuum bags and seal airtight.
3. Cook 30 minutes.
4. Add the maple syrup, bourbon, orange juice, zest and sea salt to a small saucepan and heat on medium to a simmer; reduce to a low and cook until sauce is thick.
5. Fold in the pecans and keep warm until salmon is done.
6. Remove salmon, plate, top with sauce, and serve!

Nutrition

Calories: 532 Sodium: 203 mg, Dietary Fiber: 0.3g, Fat: 12.5g, Carbs: 56.4g, Protein: 34.9g

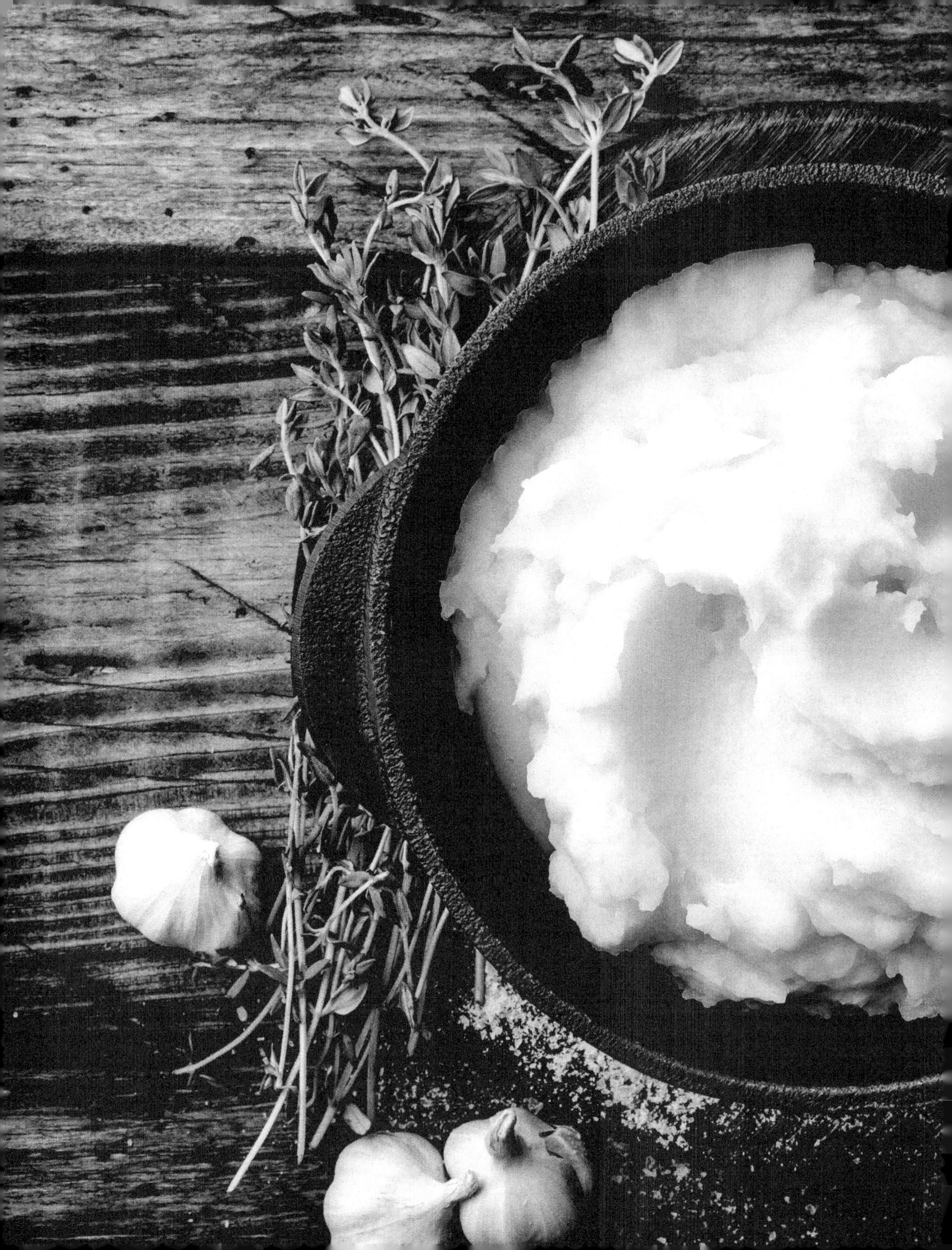

CHAPTER

9

Vegetables

& Side Dishes

Sweet Potato Infused

with Smoked Garlic, Paprika & Maple Syrup

Sweet potato infused with delicious sweet and savory spice makes for one out of this world side dish on days when you need a little comfort food.

Servings: 8
Prep time: 30 minutes
Cook time: 1 hr 15 minutes

- 2 lbs. sweet potatoes, peeled and diced
- 10 cloves garlic, smashed
- 2/3 cup salted butter
- 1 teaspoon black pepper
- 1 teaspoon cinnamon
- 1 teaspoon sea salt, plus more for serving

1. Preheat sous vide water bath to 185°F.
2. Combine all ingredients in a vacuum bag and seal.
3. Cook for 1 hour.
4. Transfer to a lined baking sheet and roast at 400°F for 15 minutes or until golden brown.
5. Serve warm with an extra pinch of salt!

Nutrition

Calories: 276 Sodium: 354 mg, Dietary Fiber: 5g, Fat: 15.6g, Carbs: 33.3g, Protein: 2.2g

Butternut Squash & Apple Soup

Calm your foodie loving soul with some deliciously warm, sweet and savory soup when you whip up this recipe!

Servings: 6
Prep time: 10 minutes
Cook time: 2 hours

- 1 medium butternut squash, peeled and sliced
- 1 large honeycrisp apple, cored and sliced
- 1/2 onion, sliced
- 1 teaspoon sea salt
- 3/4 cup light cream

1. Preheat sous vide water bath to 185°F.
2. Add squash, apple and onion to a large, one-gallon vacuum seal bag.
3. Vacuum seal the bag and remove as much air as possible.
4. Submerge the pouch in the water bath and cook for 2 hours.
5. Transfer ingredients to a blender and puree until smooth.
6. Add sea salt and cream, and puree again.
7. Serve hot!

Nutrition

Calories: 77 Sodium: 319 mg, Dietary Fiber: 1.6, Fat: 4.7g, Carbs: 9.2g, Protein: 0.8g

Sous Vide
Honey-Glazed Carrots

Honey glaze really elevates this delicious side dish to a whole new level when sous vide cooking.

Servings: 2 - 4
Prep time: 5 minutes
Cook time: 45 minutes

1 bag whole carrots, trimmed and peeled
¼ cup butter
2 tablespoons honey
1 teaspoon cinnamon
½ teaspoon sea salt

1. Preheat sous vide water bath to 185°F.
2. Combine all ingredients in a vacuum bag and seal.
3. Cook for 45 minutes.
4. Serve warm with a drizzle of the liquid from the bag.

Nutrition
Calories: 149 Sodium: 340 mg, Dietary Fiber: 1.3, Fat: 11.6g, Carbs: 12.5g, Protein: 0.5g

Rich Cream Corn
with Crispy Parmesan

Cook creamed corn with a twist when you add crispy parmesan to your delicious side dish!

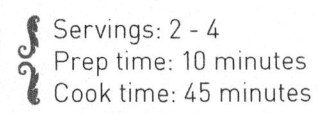

Servings: 2 - 4
Prep time: 10 minutes
Cook time: 45 minutes

4 cups fresh corn
1/2 cup heavy cream
2 tablespoons unsalted butter
2 teaspoons sugar
1 teaspoon sea salt
1/2 teaspoon white pepper

For the crispy parmesan topping:

1/2 cup panko breadcrumbs
1/4 cup Parmesan cheese
2 tablespoons unsalted butter, softened

1. Preheat a sous vide bath to 180°F.
2. Place the corn, cream, 2 tablespoons butter, sugar, salt and white pepper in a large resealable plastic bag and seal, but not airtight as corn will expand.
3. Submerge the bag into the water bath and cook for 30 minutes.
4. Transfer to a cold water bath for 5 minutes.
5. Pour the creamed corn into a frying pan.
6. Combine the topping ingredients and sprinkle evenly over the corn.
7. Bake in a 400°F oven for 15 minutes, until the topping is golden brown.
8. Allow to cool for a few minutes and serve warm.

Nutrition

Calories: 257 Sodium: 571 mg, Dietary Fiber: 4.5, Fat: 13.6g, Carbs: 33.5g, Protein: 6.2g

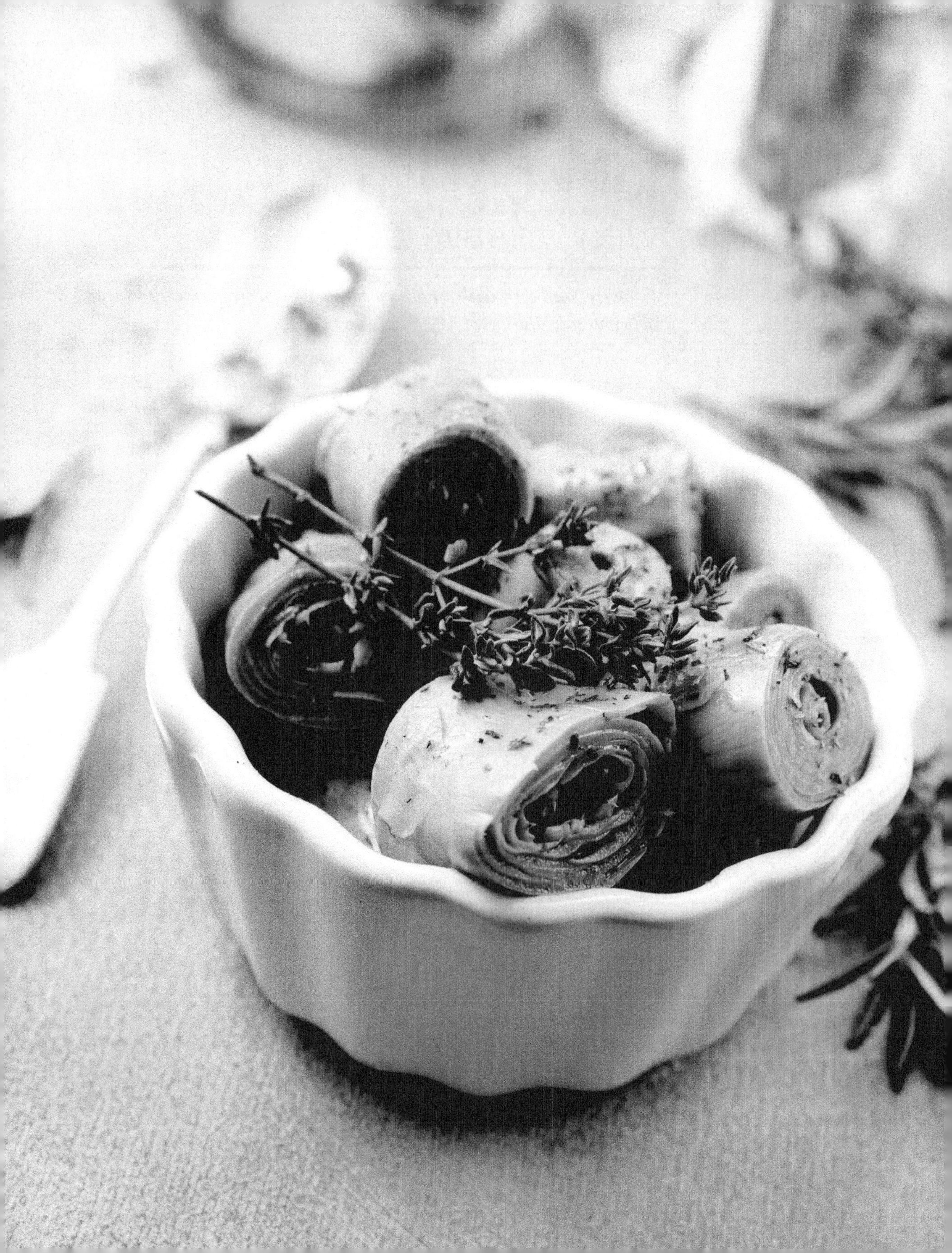

Sous Vide Artichokes

Go old world style when you cook up deliciously delicate artichokes right in your sous vide!

Servings: 2
Prep time: 20 minutes
Cook time: 1 hour

- 4 artichokes, trimmed down to their hearts
- ¼ cup premium olive oil, like Partanna
- 1 tablespoon sea salt

1. Preheat a sous vide water bath to 185°F.
2. Toss artichokes with all ingredients until well-coated in a large mixing bowl.
3. Place in a vacuum sealable bag and vacuum airtight.
4. Add to water bath and cook for 1 hour.
5. Serve immediately with your favorite dish.

Nutrition

Calories: 368 Sodium: 3113 mg, Dietary Fiber: 17.5g, Fat: 25.7g, Carbs: 34.1g, Protein: 10.6g

Doenjang-Spiced Eggplant

Eggplant has never tasted so good when you whip it up with a spicy kick in your Everie.

Servings: 2 - 4
Prep time: 5 minutes
Cook time: 45 minutes

4 large pieces of eggplant, cut into wedges
1/4 cup peanut oil
2 tablespoons doenjang paste
2 tablespoons light soy sauce
1 tablespoon brown sugar
1 tablespoon sesame seeds

1. Preheat sous vide bath to 185°F.
2. Whisk the Doenjang paste, peanut oil, soy sauce, and sugar together in a mixing bowl.
3. Add the eggplant and toss to coat evenly, then transfer to a sous vide bag and vacuum tight.
4. Cook for 45 minutes.
5. Drain the eggplant wedges from the cooking liquid.
6. Sear the eggplants on a hot grilling pan.
7. Top with sesame seeds and serve.

Nutrition
Calories: 280 Sodium: 2615 mg, Dietary Fiber: 17.1g, Fat: 15.7g, Carbs: 40.1g, Protein: 7.5g

Garlicky Brussels Sprouts

Garlic sprouts are the perfect side dish for robust and hearty meats like steak, Cornish game hens, and even duck confit!

Servings: 2
Prep time: 20 minutes
Cook time: 1 hour

1. Preheat a sous vide water bath to 185°F.
2. Add all ingredients to a resealable plastic bag and seal airtight.
3. Add to water bath and cook for 1 hour.
4. Serve immediately with your favorite dish.

- 1 lb. brussels sprouts, trimmed
- ¼ cup premium olive oil, like Partanna
- 2 tablespoons garlic, minced
- 1 tablespoon sea salt

Nutrition

Calories: 326 Sodium: 2866 mg, Dietary Fiber: 8.7g, Fat: 26g, Carbs: 23.4g, Protein: 8.3g

Creamy Mashed Potatoes
with Garlic and Rosemary

Creamy mashed potatoes with just the right amount of seasoning are the perfect side dish for your sous vide.

Servings: 10
Prep time: 25 minutes
Cook time: 2 hours

- 2 lbs. russet potatoes, sliced thin into 1/8 inch pieces
- 5 cloves garlic, peeled and smashed
- 3 sprigs rosemary
- 1 cup unsalted butter
- 1 cup whole milk
- 2 teaspoons sea salt
- 1 teaspoon black pepper

1. Preheat sous vide bath to 194°F.
2. Seal the potatoes, garlic, rosemary, butter, milk, and salt into a zip or vacuum seal bag.
3. Cook for 1 hour 30 minutes.
4. Open the bag and pour the liquid through a sieve into a small bowl and set aside for mashing.
5. Discard the rosemary.
6. Empty the potatoes into a large mixing bowl and mash with a potato ricer.
7. Gently whisk the reserved liquid back into the mashed potatoes until smooth and creamy.
8. Serve immediately.

Nutrition

Calories: 246 Sodium: 521 mg, Dietary Fiber: 2.7g, Fat: 19.5, Carbs: 16.6g, Protein: 2.7g

Tasty
Garlic Chili Tofu

Chili tofu is just the way to top your favorite salad or serve alongside your favorite roast vegetables.

Servings: 2
Prep time: 10 minutes
Cook time: 4 hours

1 block of super firm tofu
1/4 cup brown sugar
1/4 cup soy sauce
1/4 cup toasted sesame oil
2 tablespoons chili garlic paste

1. Preheat sous vide water bath to 180°F.
2. Press out liquid from tofu.
3. Cut tofu into thick chunks, about 2 inches each.
4. Preheat a frying pan on medium, spray with non-stick cooking spray, and cook until golden on each side.
5. Mix soy sauce, brown sugar, toasted sesame oil, and chili garlic paste together until well-blended in a mixing bowl.
6. Toss tofu in sauce to coat well.
7. Transfer tofu and sauce to a resealable plastic bag and seal.
8. Submerge in sous vide bath and cook for 4 hours.
9. Remove and serve immediately.

Nutrition

Calories: 377 Sodium: 1842 mg, Dietary Fiber: 1.3g, Fat: 29.8g, Carbs: 21.7g, Protein: 7g

Naturally Delicious
Asparagus

Sous vide asparagus goes perfectly alongside those creamy garlic and rosemary infused mashed potatoes every night of the week.

Servings: 2 - 4
Prep time: 5 minutes
Cook time: 1 hour

- 1 lb. asparagus, cleaned and dried with a paper towel
- 2 teaspoons olive oil
- 1 tablespoon garlic powder
- 1 teaspoon sea salt

Nutrition

Calories: 50 Sodium: 471mg, Dietary Fiber: 2.6g, Fat: 2.5, Carbs: 5.9g, Protein: 2.8g

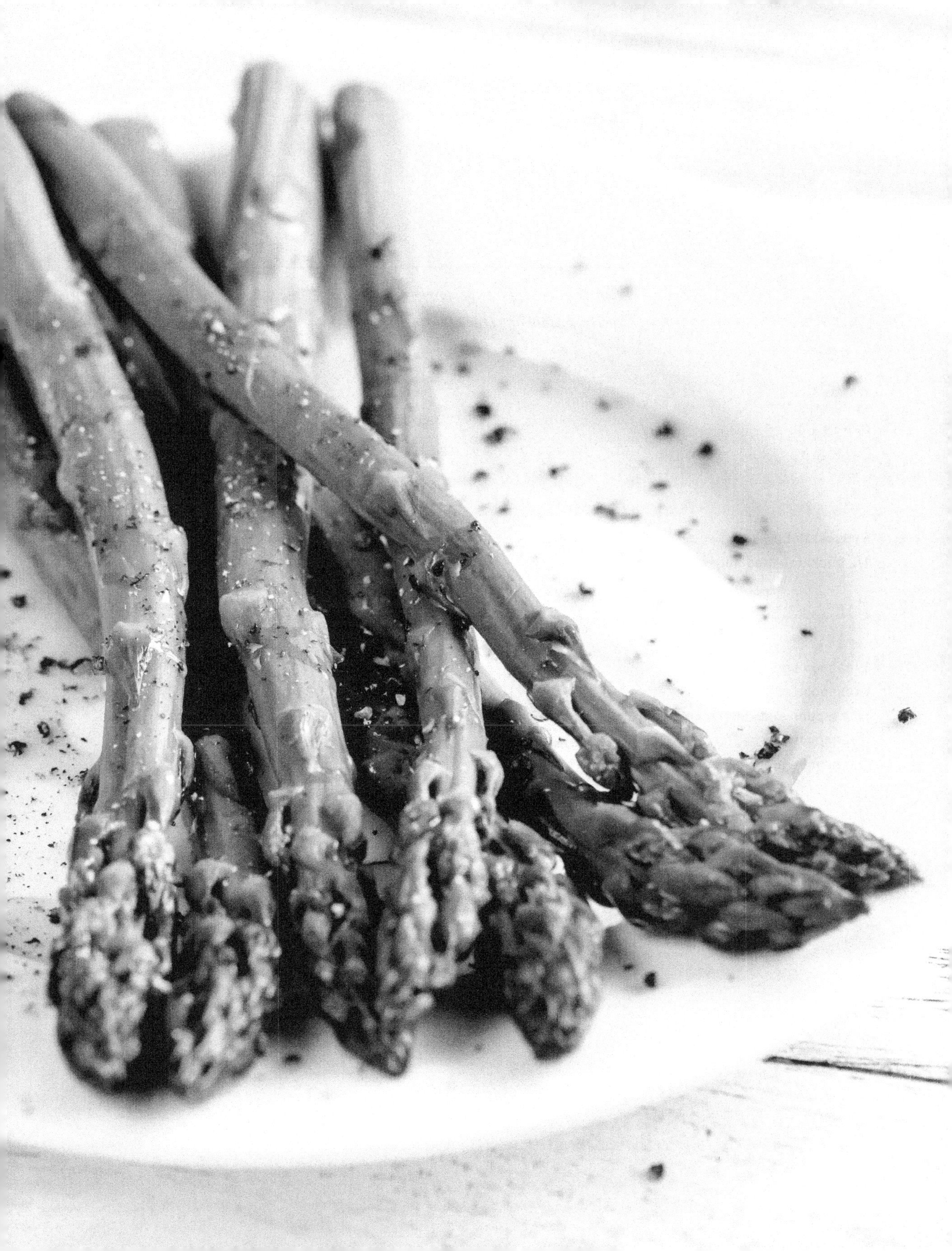

Yummy Steak Fries

Yummy steak fries go perfect with any burger, so why not sous vide them while you've got the meat on the grill!

Servings: 2 - 4
Prep time: 10 minutes
Cook time: 1 hour 35 minutes

5 russet Potatoes
1/2 stick unsalted butter

For the seasoning mix:

1 teaspoon garlic powder
1 teaspoon chili powder
½ teaspoon smoked paprika
½ teaspoon sea salt
½ teaspoon black pepper

1. Preheat a sous vide bath to 190°F.
2. Cut potatoes in half and lengthwise into wedges.
3. Melt butter in the microwave.
4. Mix together seasonings in a separate bowl.
5. Place potatoes in a resealable plastic bag, toss in butter until covered evenly.
6. Toss in seasoning mix and toss to coat again.
7. Seal and lower bag into the water bath
8. Cook for 90 minutes.
9. Remove, place on a baking sheet broil for 2-3 minutes on each side.
10. Serve hot!

Nutrition

Calories: 291 Sodium: 388 mg, Dietary Fiber: 6.9g, Fat: 11.9g, Carbs: 43g, Protein: 4.9g

Uni Chawanmushi

An Asian delicacy, this custard is the perfect side dish for Pho or grilled fish with vegetables.

Servings: 4
Prep time: 10 minutes
Cook time: 1 hour

2 teaspoons instant dashi powder
2 cups warm water
3 large eggs
4 (8 ounce) mason jars

For the topping:

4 pieces fresh sea urchin (uni)
Dulse flakes, to garnish
1 small truffle, shaved
Chervil leaves, to garnish
Finishing salt

1. Preheat sous vide water bath to 176°F.
2. Whisk dashi powder and warm water together in a mixing bowl until dashi is dissolved; set aside to rest.
3. Gently whisk eggs until blended in a separate mixing bowl; do not incorporate too much air to avoid bubbles.
4. Gently fold in the dashi broth.
5. Slowly pour the chawanmushi base into mason jars being careful not to create any air bubbles.
6. Seal lid tightly and place into water bath with tongs.
7. Cook for 1 hour.
8. Gently remove from water bath with tongs.
9. Top with dulse flakes, a piece of uni, chervil leaves, shaved truffles, and a pinch of finishing salt - and enjoy!

Nutrition

Calories: 146 Sodium: 191 mg, Dietary Fiber: 1g, Fat: 8.6g, Carbs: 8.4g, Protein: 7.9g

Garlic Cheese Risotto

Velvety smooth risotto is the way to dress up any stuffed pork chop or serve alongside your favorite Italian inspired main dishes.

Servings: 4
Prep time: 5 minutes
Cook time: 45 minutes

- 1 cup Arborio rice
- 1 teaspoon premium olive oil, like Partanna
- 2 tablespoons roasted minced garlic
- 3 cups chicken or vegetable broth
- Pinch of sea salt
- Pinch of black pepper
- 1/3 cup grated Romano cheese

1. Preheat a sous vide water bath to 183°F.
2. Add all ingredients but cheese to a resealable plastic bag and seal.
3. Submerge the bag in the water bath and cook for 45 minutes.
4. Remove from the water bath and add risotto to a mixing bowl.
5. Fold in cheese until well-incorporated and serve warm.

Nutrition

Calories: 366 Sodium: 166 mg, Dietary Fiber: 1.3g, Fat: 6.5g, Carbs: 39.4g, Protein: 34.3g

Fluffy Sushi Rice

Perfectly fluffy sushi rice is just the thing to whip up in order to make the most out of your time and your Everie.

Servings: 25
Prep time: 25 minutes
Cook time: 45 minutes

2 cups sushi rice
1/4 cup mirin
1/4 cup white wine vinegar
1/4 cup granulated sugar
2 tablespoons sea salt

1. Preheat water bath to 200°F.
2. Rinse rice by placing it in a mixing bowl and covering with lukewarm water; rub the rice through your fingers until the water is white with excess starch.
3. Strain using colander; repeat 4 more times.
4. Allow rice to dry in colander for 15 minutes.
5. Bring 2 cups of water to a rolling boil on high heat.
6. Add rice and water to a heavy resealable plastic bag.
7. Seal, but don't vacuum as rice will expand.
8. Submerge in water bath and cook for 45 minutes.
9. Combine vinegars, sugar and salt in a small saucepan.
10. Bring to boil until sugar and salt dissolve.
11. Transfer the rice to a large mixing bowl.
12. Sprinkle 1/2 cup of the seasoned vinegar over the rice.
13. Fold to combine with a rubber spatula, drizzling with remaining vinegar mixture.
14. Gently separate the rice grains while mixing in the seasoning.
15. Use to roll sushi or as the base of nigiri.

Nutrition

Calories: 66 Sodium: 470 mg, Dietary Fiber: 0.2g, Fat: 0.1g, Carbs: 15g, Protein: 1.1g

Delicate and Tasty Mushrooms

Earthy mushrooms cook up perfectly when you sous vide them and serve with everything.

Servings: 4
Prep Time: 10 minutes
Cook Time: 30 minutes

- 1 lb. button mushrooms cleaned, rinsed, and cut into bite-size pieces
- 2 tablespoons soy sauce
- 2 tablespoons extra-virgin olive oil
- 1 tablespoon balsamic vinegar
- 1/2 teaspoon black pepper
- 1/2 teaspoon sea salt, plus more to taste

1. Preheat your sous vide water bath to 176°F.
2. Combine the mushrooms with the rest of the ingredients, in a large mixing bowl, and toss to coat evenly.
3. Place the mixture in a sealable plastic bag; seal using the water displacement method or use a vacuum sealer.
4. Add mushrooms to the water bath and cook for 30 minutes.
5. Remove the bag from the water bath and serve immediately with your favorite meal.

Nutrition

Calories: 90 Sodium: 692 mg, Dietary Fiber: 1.3g, Fat: 7.3g, Carbs: 4.5g, Protein: 4.1g

Rich and Hearty
Polenta

Polenta is a beautiful rice alternative that can be whipped up in a sous vide and really become the star of any meal you serve it with!

Servings: 4 - 6
Prep time: 5 minutes
Cook time: 1 hour

- 1/2 cup dry yellow polenta
- 2 cups chicken or vegetable stock
- ¼ cup butter, unsalted
- Sea salt
- ¼ cup pecorino romano cheese, for serving

1. Preheat sous vide water bath to 182°F.
2. Add polenta, stock, butter and a pinch of sea salt to a resealable plastic bag and seal.
3. Submerge the bag in the water bath and cook for 1 hour.
4. Remove from the water bath and add to a mixing bowl.
5. Fold in cheese until well-incorporated and serve warm.

Nutrition
Calories: 176 Sodium: 233 mg, Dietary Fiber: 0.1g, Fat: 10.7g, Carbs: 3.6g, Protein: 15.8g

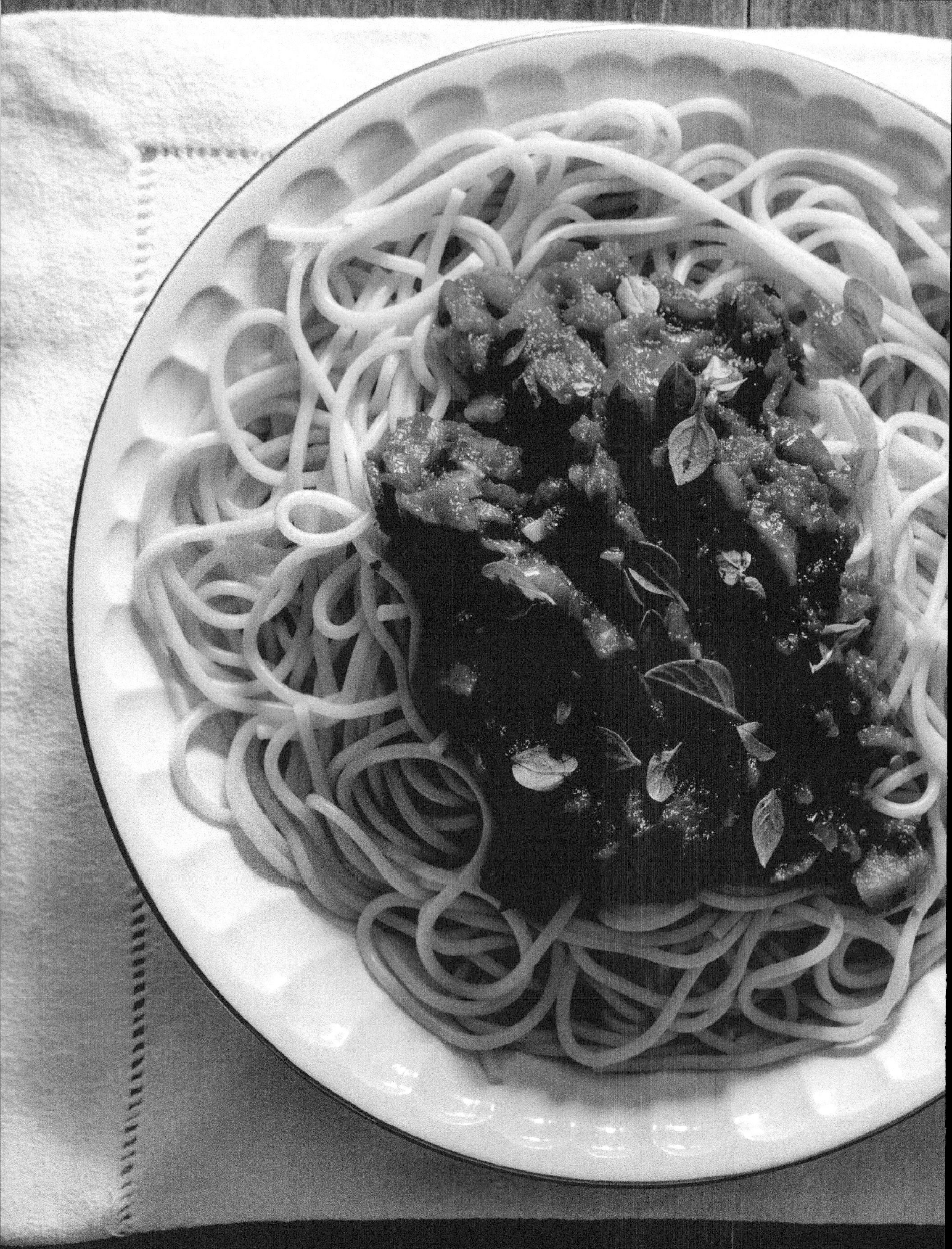

CHAPTER 10

Sauces
& Condiments

Creamy Hollandaise Sauce

Creamy hollandaise sauce is the perfect decadent topping for eggs and vegetables alike and you can prepare it easily in your sous vide.

Servings: 2 - 4
Prep time: 5 minutes
Cook time: 1 hour

2 tablespoons fresh lemon juice
2 tablespoons water
2 egg yolks
1 stick butter
Salt
Pepper

1. Preheat sous vide water bath to 147°F.
2. Add all of the ingredients to a resealable plastic bag, and squeeze to break up the egg yolks, and seal airtight.
3. Submerge the bag in the water bath and cook for 1 hour.
4. Remove hollandaise from the water bath and pour into a wide bottom container.
5. Use an immersion blender to blend the layers out of the hollandaise sauce until you have a velvet smooth texture, and the sauce clings to a spoon.
6. Store refrigerated in a mason jar and warm in a hot water bath to serve.

Nutrition

Calories: 231 Sodium: 207 mg, Dietary Fiber: 0g, Fat: 25.2g, Carbs: 0.5g, Protein: 1.7g

Sous Vide
Flavor-Packed Pickles

Easy to make, flavor packed pickles are a lovely way to put your Everie sous vide to use when making condiments at home.

Servings: 10
Prep time: 10 minutes
Cook time: 2 hrs 30 minutes, plus overnight for brining

20 small cucumbers, stems removed
4 medium mason jars
20 black peppercorns
4 garlic cloves, smashed
4 teaspoons fresh dill

For the Pickling Brine:

2 ½ cups white wine vinegar
2 ½ cups water
½ cup sugar, granulated
2 tablespoons pickling salt

1. Preheat sous vide bath to 140°F.
2. Whisk brine ingredients together in a large mixing bowl until well-combined.
3. Place 5 cucumbers, 5 peppercorns, 1 garlic clove, and 1 teaspoon dill in each mason jar.
4. Fill each jar with brine and seal lid tight.
5. Submerge mason jars in water bath and cook for 2 hours 30 minutes.
6. Remove from the water bath and allow to cool to room temperature.
7. Refrigerate overnight or up to 3 days to brine.
8. Serve with your favorite meals or as a delicious snack.

Nutrition

Calories: 475 Sodium: 1422 mg, Dietary Fiber: 0.9g, Fat: 27.8g, Carbs: 49.9g, Protein: 4.7g

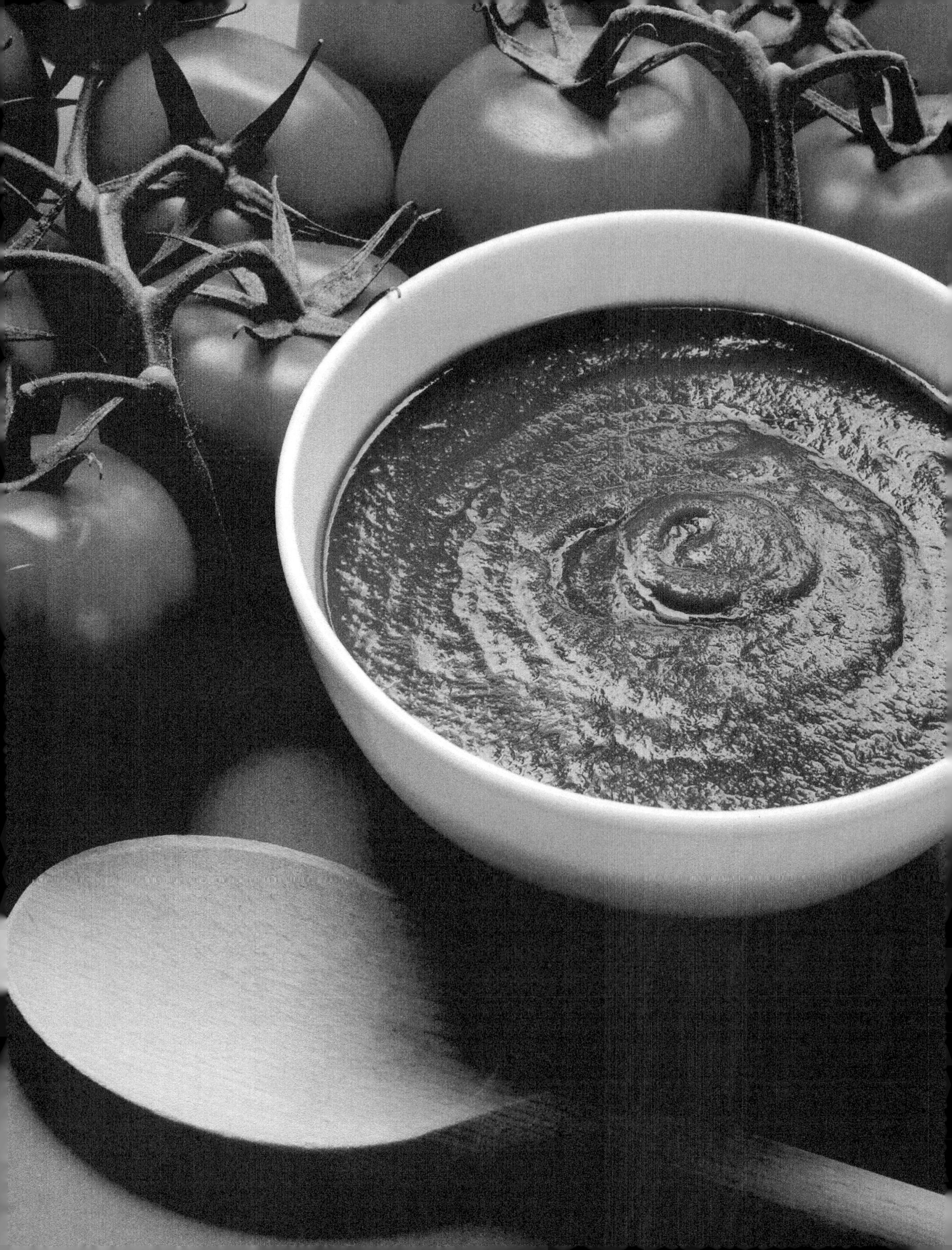

Easy Rich
Tomato Sauce

Whipping up your very own tomato sauce is so very easy with the sous vide, so you can enjoy your summer garden for quick evening meals all winter long.

Servings: 4 - 6
Prep time: 10 minutes
Cook time: 55 minutes

- 2 tablespoons olive oil
- 1/2 cup onion, chopped
- 2 garlic cloves, minced
- 3 sprigs fresh oregano, stemmed
- 2 pounds ripe tomatoes
- 6 large basil leaves, chopped
- 1 whole green pepper, seeded and cut into four large pieces

Nutrition

Nutritional Info: Calories: 84 Sodium: 9 mg, Dietary Fiber: 3.4g, Fat: 5.3g, Carbs: 9.5g, Protein: 2g

Tangy Southwest
Pickled Onions

Pickled onions are a delicious summer time snack served with potato chips and mixed nuts, or use them to give your favorite salads a tangy punch.

Servings: 10
Prep time: 5 minutes
Cook time: 2 hrs 30 minutes, plus overnight for brining

6 - 8 red onions, julienned

For the brine:

2 cups fresh lime juice
2 cups tequila
¼ cup sugar
1 teaspoon chipotle powder
1 teaspoon cumin
1 teaspoon pickling salt

1. Preheat sous vide bath to 140°F.
2. Whisk brine ingredients together in a large mixing bowl until well-combined.
3. Distribute onions evenly to mason jars.
4. Fill each jar with brine.
5. Submerge mason jars in water bath and cook for 2 hours 30 minutes.
6. Remove from the water bath and allow to cool to room temperature.
7. Refrigerate overnight or up to 3 days to brine.
8. Serve with your favorite meals or as a delicious snack.

Nutrition

Calories: 183 Sodium: 236 mg, Dietary Fiber: 1.5g, Fat: 1.8g, Carbs: 12g, Protein: 2.8g

Hot Chili Chutney

For all things curry and Indian dishes at home, you'll love this hot chili chutney that is the perfect complement to crisp poppadoms and cool raita.

Servings: 6
Prep time: 10 minutes
Cook time: 5 hrs 50 minutes

5 medium jalapeños
2 medium red bell peppers
1 medium red onion, chopped
1/2 tablespoon rosemary
1 bay leaf
1/2 teaspoon ground cinnamon
1/4 teaspoon sea salt
1/4 teaspoon black pepper
1/2 cup brown sugar
1 tablespoon balsamic vinegar

1. Preheat sous vide bath to 182°F.
2. Roast the peppers under a broiler until skins are completely charred.
3. Transfer the peppers to a bowl, cover with plastic wrap, and let sit about 15 to 20 minutes or until cool enough to handle.
4. Peel away the charred outer skins, cut the peppers in half, core, seed, and finely chop the flesh.
5. Add peppers and remaining ingredients to a cooking pouch and vacuum seal.
6. Submerge the pouch in water bath and cook for 5 hours.
7. Remove from the water bath and quick chill by submerging in ice water for 30 minutes.
8. Serve right away, or refrigerate in the pouch, unopened, for up to a week.

Nutrition

Calories: 91 Sodium: 84 mg, Dietary Fiber: 3.3g, Fat: 0.6g, Carbs: 21.5g, Protein: 1.7g

Holiday
Cranberry Sauce

Cranberry sauce is the perfect complement to poultry like turkey or Cornish hens served with stuffing and mashed potatoes.

Servings: 6 - 8
Prep time: 3 minutes
Cook time: 2 hours

1 package frozen cranberries (or fresh)
1-2 tablespoons raw honey
3 drops cinnamon oil
1 drop clove oil
1 drop orange oil
½ tablespoon cinnamon
½ teaspoon nutmeg
1 cinnamon stick

1. Preheat water bath to 185°F.
2. Place cranberries in a sealed bag along with remaining ingredients and cook for about 2 hours.
3. Remove and transfer to an ice bath for 5 - 10 minutes.
4. Serve with your favorite meals; alternatively you can refrigerate for up to 14 days.

Nutrition
Calories: 98 Sodium: 0mg, Dietary Fiber: 2.8g, Fat: 5.4g, Carbs: 9g, Protein: 0g

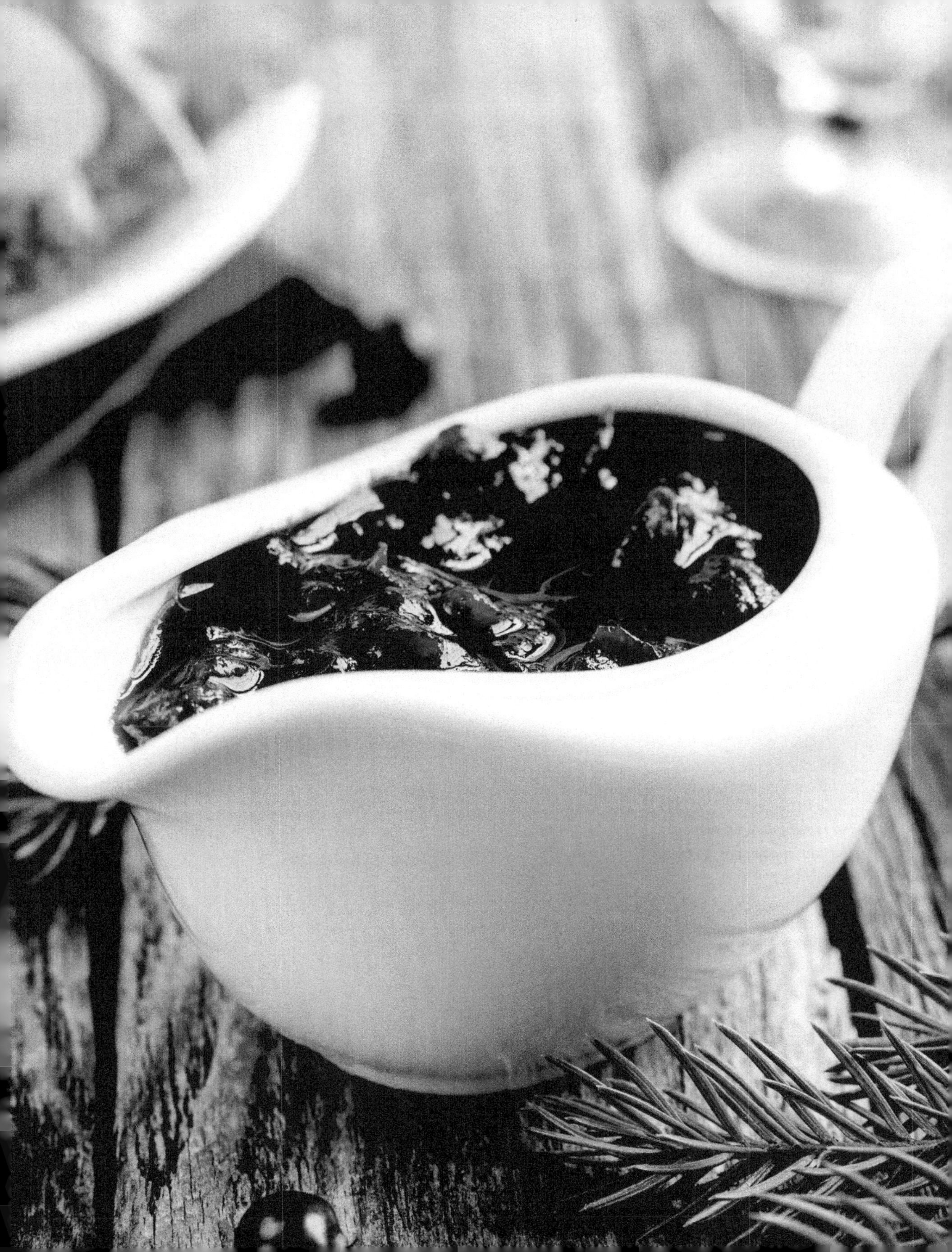

Creamy Béarnaise Sauce

Known as baby hollandaise, this sauce is easy to make and perfect served atop your favorite cut of steak and fingerling potatoes for one decadent touch.

Servings: 2 - 4
Prep time: 15 minutes
Cook time: 30 minutes

For the reduction:

1 bunch fresh tarragon, chopped
2 medium shallots, minced
½ cup white wine vinegar
½ cup dry white wine
6 whole black peppercorns

For the sauce:

3 egg yolks
2 cups, premium French butter, like President
3-4 tablespoons reduction
Sea salt and pepper, to taste

1. Preheat water bath for 140°F.
2. In a small saucepan, combine tarragon, shallots, vinegar, pepper and wine over medium-high heat.
3. Bring to simmer and cook until reduced by half.
4. Remove from heat, strain liquid, and set it aside to cool.
5. Place reduction, butter and egg yolks in a resealable plastic bag - DO NOT seal.
6. Place the bag in the water bath to cook for 30 minutes.
7. Pour the sauce into a food processor or blender, and process until thickened.
8. Season with sea salt and pepper, and serve immediately.

Nutrition

Calories: 205 Sodium: 89 mg, Dietary Fiber: 1.5g, Fat: 6.4g, Carbs: 26.9g, Protein: 5.7g

Classic Pickled Onions

Classic pickled onions are absolutely delicious, and you can even pickled sliced carrots and cauliflower for delicious giardiniera with this recipe!

Servings: 10
Prep time: 5 minutes
Cook time: 2 hrs 30 minutes, plus overnight for brining

6 cups pearl onions

For the Pickling Brine:

2 cups white vinegar
½ cup dry white wine
2 ½ cups water
½ cup sugar, granulated
2 tablespoons pickling salt

1. Preheat sous vide bath to 140°F.
2. Whisk brine ingredients together in a large mixing bowl until well-combined.
3. Distribute onions evenly into mason jars, but leave loose for brine.
4. Fill each jar with brine.
5. Submerge mason jars in water bath and cook for 2 hours 30 minutes.
6. Remove from the water bath and allow to cool to room temperature.
7. Refrigerate overnight or up to 3 days to brine.
8. Serve with your favorite meals or as a delicious snack.

Nutrition

Calories: 85 Sodium: 1160 mg, Dietary Fiber: 1.5g, Fat: 0.1g, Carbs: 17.2g, Protein: 0.8g

Spicy Pickled Pineapple

Sweet meets spice for a perfect pineapple treat in this sous vide recipe.

Servings: 6
Prep time: 5 minutes
Cook time: 30 minutes, plus overnight for brining

- 1 cup jalapeño peppers, seeded and chopped
- 2 cups fresh pineapple, cut in 2 inch squares
- 1 large red onion, julienned
- 1 teaspoon pickling spice
- 1 1/2 teaspoon pickling salt
- 1/3 cup apple cider vinegar

1. Fill the Everie with water and set to 140°F.
2. Add all ingredients to a sealable bag and seal airtight.
3. Place in water bath and cook for 30 minutes.
4. Transfer to mason jar and refrigerate overnight to brine.
5. Serve chilled with your favorite meals!

Nutrition
Calories: 45 Sodium: 772 mg, Dietary Fiber: 1.8g, Fat: 0.3g, Carbs: 10.5g, Protein: 0.7g

Pickled Husk Cherries

Pickled husk cherries are the perfect treat to make with your Everie that is out of this world delicious.

Servings: 10
Prep time: 5 minutes
Cook time: 45 minutes, plus overnight for brining

1 pint husk cherries, hulled
1 cup white vinegar
2 cups water
2 teaspoons black peppercorns
1 teaspoon coriander seeds
2 sprigs fresh thyme
6 whole cloves
½ cup brown sugar
1 teaspoon salt

1. Preheat sous vide to 140°F.
2. Combine all of the ingredients, except for the cherries, in a large pot and bring the brine to a boil.
3. Remove from heat and let it cool to below 140°F.
4. Place the hulled husk cherries in a resealable plastic bag with the brine, seal airtight, and cook for 45 minutes in sous vide bath.
5. Remove and allow cherries to cool to room temperature.
6. Refrigerate in brine overnight, up to a few days, and enjoy.

Nutrition

Calories: 57 Sodium: 249 mg, Dietary Fiber: 1.8g, Fat: 0.9g, Carbs: 12.6g, Protein: 0.4g

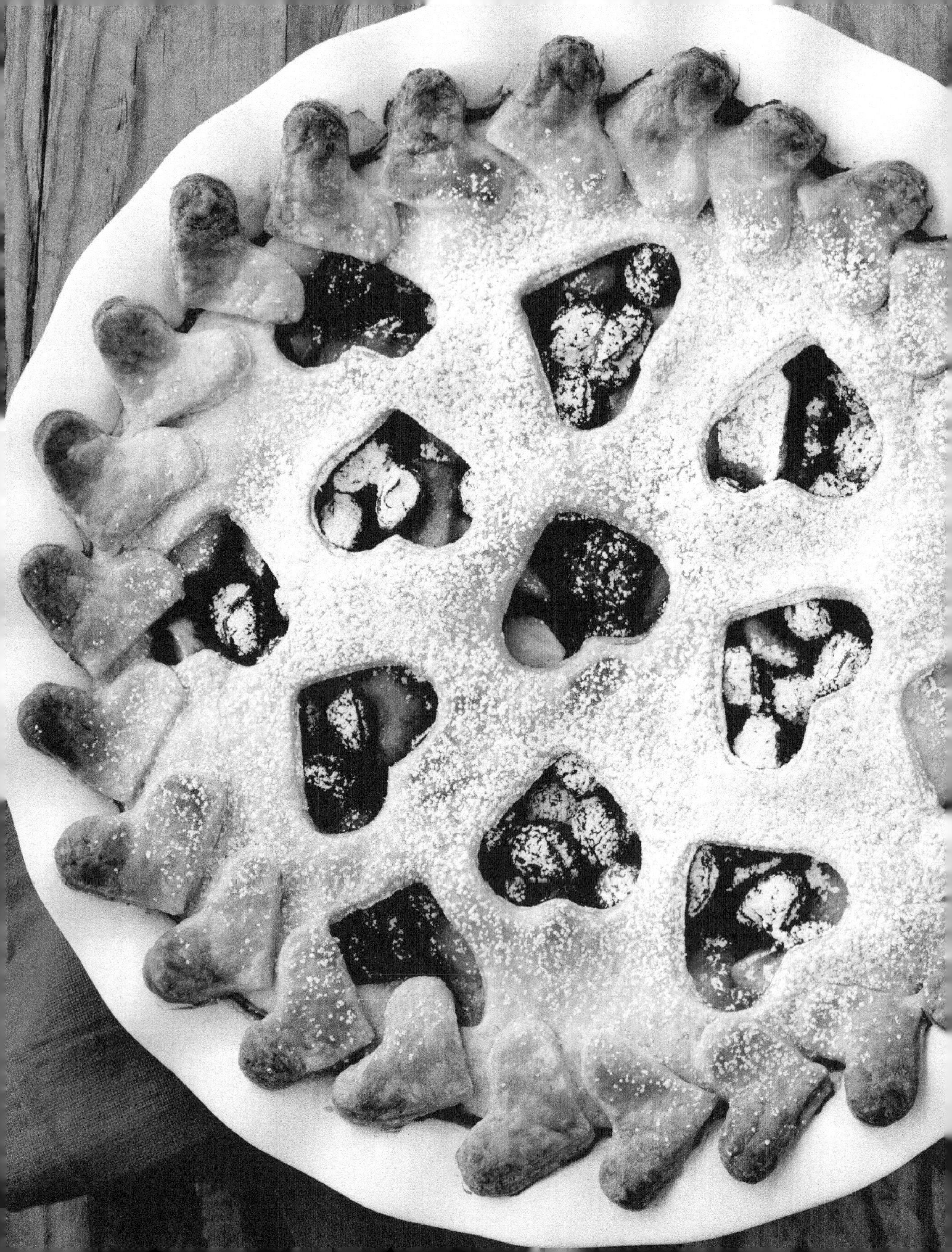

CHAPTER 11

Desserts

Apple Cranberry Pie page 136

Easy Sous Vide Dulce De Leche

Decadent Dulce De Leche is the perfect way to whip up dessert for friends and family sous vide style.

Servings: 4
Prep Time: 10 minutes
Cook Time: 15 hours

4 (14 ounce) cans of sweetened condensed milk

4 Clean, sterilized (4-8 oz.) canning jars with lids

1. Fill the sous vide container with water to just below the max fill line.
2. Preheat water to 185°F.
3. Pour the sweetened condensed milk into jars, leaving 1 inch of space at the top; screw each lid on tight.
4. Immerse the jars in the Everie.
5. Add more water, if needed, to cover the tops of the jars; do not fill over the max fill line.
6. Cook for 15 hours, or until the dessert is thick and a dark caramel color.
7. Remove the jars and cool to room temperature and enjoy; alternatively it will keep in the refrigerator for up to 3 months.

Nutrition
Calories: 1274 Sodium: 504 mg, Dietary Fiber: 0g, Fat: 34.5g, Carbs: 215.9g, Protein: 31.4g

Yummy Flourless Chocolate Cake

For those who love flourless desserts, this yummy chocolate cake is just the way to finish a beautiful dinner or compliment your favorite hot drink in the afternoon.

Servings: 6
Prep time: 10 minutes
Cook time: 7 hour 15 minutes

4 large eggs, cold
½ pound semisweet chocolate chips
4 ounces butter
6 (4 ounce) mason jars
Powdered sugar, for dusting cakes

1. Place chocolate and butter in a resealable freezer bag and place in the water bath for 15 minutes to melt chocolate; massage the bag every 5 minutes to ensure the mixture is well blended.
2. Remove the bag and set the sous vide to 170°F.
3. Spray mason jars with non-stick spray or grease with butter.
4. Beat the eggs with a standing mixer at high speed until the volume doubles.
5. Turn the mixer to low, cut the corner off the freezer bag, and drizzle the melted chocolate mixture in slowly until the mixture is totally homogeneous.
6. Scrape the batter into canning jars and smooth the surface by tapping the jar firmly but gently on a flat surface.
7. Screw each lid on tight and add jars carefully to your water bath for 60 minutes.
8. Cool jars on a wire rack to room temperature.
9. Place jars in the refrigerator, cover with a kitchen towel, and leave to set for 6 hours.
10. Garnish with powdered sugar to serve.

Nutrition

Calories: 375 Sodium: 156 mg, Dietary Fiber: 2g, Fat: 29.3g, Carbs: 25.6g, Protein: 4.4g

Decadent Leche Flan

Sweet creme caramel is the most delicious way to fill your flan and can be made right at home in your Everie sous vide container.

Servings: 6
Prep time: 15 minutes
Cook time: 2 hours

3/4 cup granulated sugar
12 egg yolks
1 (14 ounce) can condensed milk
1 (12 ounce) can evaporated milk
1 teaspoon pure vanilla extract
6 (4 ounce) mason glass jars

1. Preheat water bath to 180°F.
2. Heat sugar in a saucepan over medium heat until liquified to a dark, caramel brown color. Pour equal portions into mason jars and set aside to cool.
3. Combine yolks, milk, vanilla extract and gently stir; do not whip or beat.
4. Strain, with a cheesecloth, evenly, into each mason jar; leave just enough room for the lid to close tightly.
5. Add to Everie for 2 hours.
6. Remove to cool slowly to room temperature.
7. Refrigerate overnight and serve chilled.

Nutrition

Calories: 492 Sodium: 160 mg, Dietary Fiber: 0g, Fat: 19.1g, Carbs: 68g, Protein: 14.5g

Vanilla
Creme Brûlée

Creamy creme brûlée is just delicious when cooked sous vide style.

Servings: 8
Prep time: 25 minutes
Cook time: 1 hour

10 large egg yolks
½ cup sugar
3 cups heavy whipping cream
1 vanilla bean pod, split and scraped
8 (4 ounce) canning jars

1. Preheat water to 176°F.
2. Add cream, vanilla pod and seeds to a saucepan, bring to a boil, remove from heat, cover, and let rest for 15 minutes.
3. Whisk egg yolks and sugar in a mixing bowl until it's a pale yellow.
4. Remove the vanilla bean pod from the cream.
5. Add the cream a little at a time to the egg yolk mixture, whisking continually.
6. Pour the liquid into eight 4 ounce jars and place the lid on the jar.
7. Tighten the lids until they just closed in order to allow the jars to release air bubbles while cooking.
8. Carefully place jars in sous vide.
9. Cook for 1 hour.
10. Once done, remove from water and allow to cool at room temperature for 30 minutes.
11. After cooling, place in fridge for at least 1 hour or up to 2 days.
12. About 30 minutes before serving, remove from fridge.
13. Just before serving remove lids and sprinkle about a teaspoon of sugar onto the custard.
14. Torch the sugar until it has caramelized and serve immediately.

Nutrition

Calories: 290 Sodium: 29 mg, Dietary Fiber: 0.8g, Fat: 23.8g, Carbs: 17.4g, Protein: 4.8g

Gooey Chocolate Chip Cookies

If you love cookies, you'll love this ooey gooey chocolate chip cookie recipe for the sous vide.

Servings: 24
Prep time: 10 minutes
Cook time: 4 hours

1 cup all-purpose flour
1 teaspoon baking powder
1/4 teaspoon sea salt
6 tablespoons unsalted butter, at room temperature
2/3 cup dark brown sugar, packed
1 large egg
2 teaspoons vanilla extract
1 cup chocolate chip cookies
Unsalted butter, for greasing

1. Preheat water to 195°F.
2. Generously grease 5 half pint canning jars with unsalted butter.
3. Whisk flour, baking powder, and salt together in a mixing bowl and set aside.
4. Combine butter and sugar in a separate mixing bowl with an electric mixer; beat the mixture on medium-high speed until light and fluffy, about 3 to 5 minutes.
5. Fold in the egg, followed by the vanilla, and continue to beat until mixture is very light and fluffy; about 3 additional minutes.
6. Gently fold in the flour mixture until just combined.
7. Fold in the chocolate chips.
8. Divide the dough between the prepared jars.
9. Pat dough down to the bottom of the jars with lightly buttered fingers; each jar should be no more than half full.
10. Wipe off sides and tops of jars using a damp towel.
11. Place lids and bands on jars and seal until just tight; do not over-tighten jars.
12. Place jars in water bath and set the timer for 3 hours.
13. Remove the jars from the water bath.
14. Place on a cooling rack. Carefully remove the lids and let the cookies cool to room temperature.
15. Run a knife around the sides of the jars and carefully transfer to a plate. Refrigerate until chilled, about 1 hour.
16. Slice each cookie into 1/4-inch thick slices and serve.

Nutrition

Calories: 74 Sodium: 51 mg, Dietary Fiber: 0.1g, Fat: 3.7g, Carbs: 9.3g, Protein: 0.9g

Mason Jar
Salted Caramel Cheesecake

Creamy cheesecake is also possible right in the heart of your kitchen with sous vide.

Servings: 4
Prep time: 15 minutes
Cook time: 90 minutes

- 1 cup graham cracker crumbs
- 1 tablespoon unsalted butter, room temperature
- 1 (8 ounce) package neufchatel cheese
- 1 1/2 cups Greek vanilla yogurt, strained
- 1/4 cup water
- 1 (.25-ounce) packet unflavored gelatin
- 8 (4 ounce) mason jars

For the caramel sauce:
- 1 cup sugar
- 6 tablespoons unsalted butter
- 1/2 cup heavy cream
- Sea salt, for serving

1. Preheat water bath to 176°F.
2. Blend graham cracker crumbs and the butter together in a mixing bowl to make cheesecake crust.
3. Spoon mixture evenly into each mason jar and press to form the crust.
4. Whip the Greek yogurt and cream cheese together in a mixing bowl, with a hand mixer, until smooth.
5. Bring water to a boil and add the unflavored gelatin, whisking until it is dissolved and smooth.
6. Add the warm gelatin to the cheesecake batter slowly, whipping until smooth.
7. Add batter evenly to mason jars, screw lids on tight, and place in water bath for 90 minutes.
8. Remove cheese cakes and refrigerate for at least 4 hours or overnight to set.
9. Prepare the sauce by adding the sugar to a saucepan over medium heat; whisk until the sugar has completely melted, turning into a rich, gold liquid.
10. Remove from heat and whisk in the butter.
11. Stream in the cream slowly, whisking until the caramel sauce comes together; pour into a glass jar and let cool.
12. Top each mini cheesecake with the caramel sauce and a touch of sea salt for serving.

Nutrition
Calories: 577 Sodium: 624 mg, Dietary Fiber: 1.3g, Fat: 24.8g, Carbs: 75.9g, Protein: 14.1g

Delicate Honey Lavender
Poached Peaches

The perfect after dinner dessert, lavender laced sweet peaches will surely calm the senses after a lovely evening.

Servings: 4
Prep time: 10 minutes
Cook time: 20 minutes

2 peaches, halved and pitted
1 tablespoon dried lavender
¼ cup water
¼ cup honey
Plain yogurt, for serving

1. Preheat water to 185°F in your Everie.
2. Add the peaches to a small 1 quart cooking pouch.
3. Sprinkle in the lavender and pour in the water and honey.
4. Remove the air and zip the seal.
5. Submerge the pouch in the water and cook for 20 minutes.
6. Remove from the water bath and add to an ice water bath and refrigerate for one hour.
7. Spoon the peaches into a bowl.
8. Sieve the poaching liquid into each bowl and discard the lavender buds.
9. Serve with a dollop of plain yogurt.

Nutrition

Calories: 143 Sodium: 6 mg, Dietary Fiber: 1.8g, Fat: 3.7g, Carbs: 28g, Protein: 1.7g

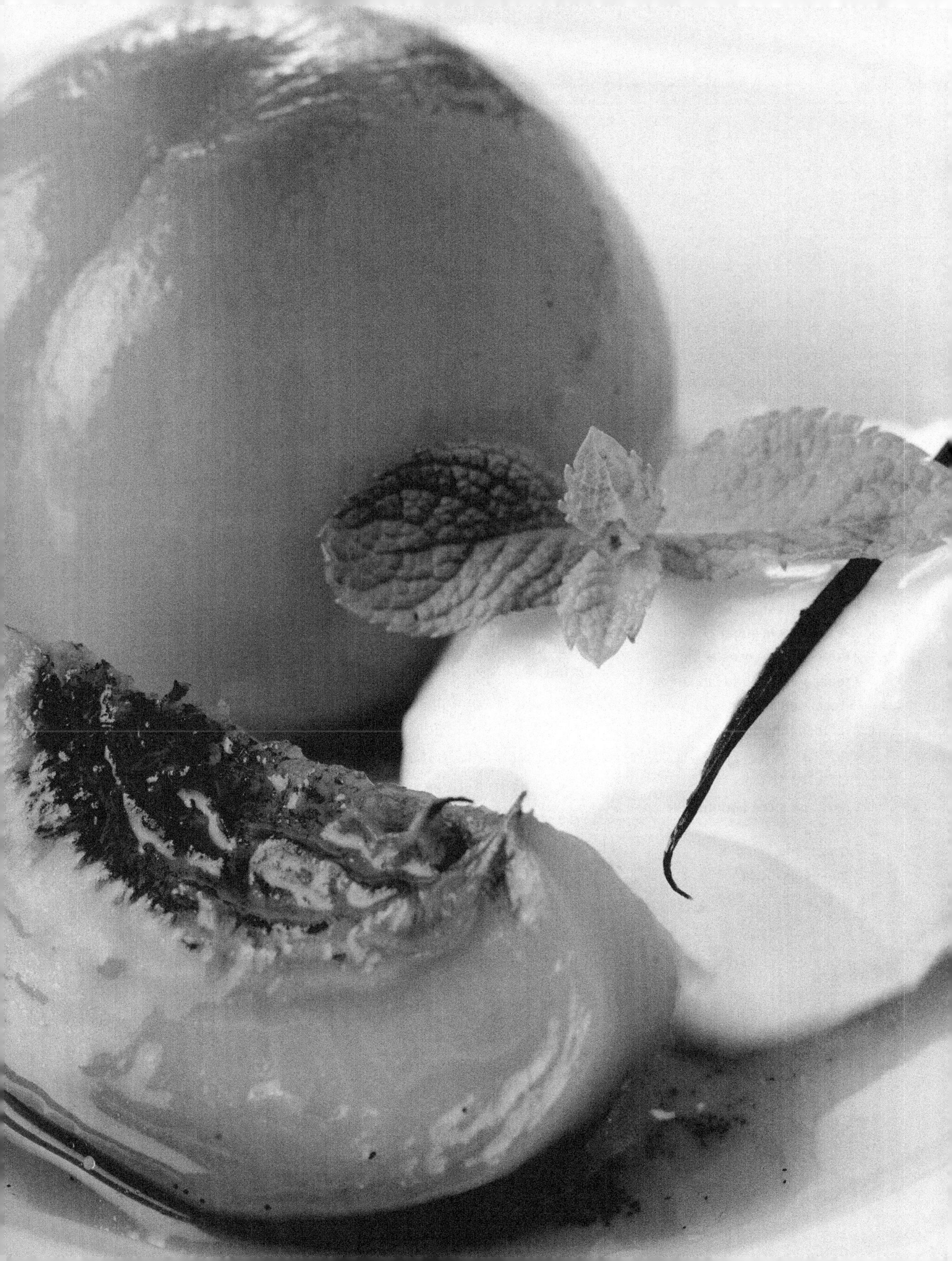

Apple Cranberry Pie

Decadent apple pie can be whipped up in no time when it comes to sous vide cooking.

Servings: 4
Prep time: 5 minutes
Cook time: 2 hrs 15 minutes

2 pounds honey crisp apples, peeled, cored and diced 1/4 inch chunks
8 ounces fresh cranberries
3/4 cup brown sugar
2 tablespoons cornstarch
2 teaspoons ground cinnamon
½ teaspoon nutmeg
2 tablespoons butter

For the pie crust:

1 package store bought puff pastry
2 teaspoons 2% milk
2 teaspoons sugar

1. Preheat a water bath to 160°F.
2. Add apples, cranberries, brown sugar, cornstarch, ground cinnamon, nutmeg, and butter to a resealable plastic bag; use the water displacement to get the air out and seal.
3. Place the sealed bag in the water bath for 90 minutes.
4. Plunge the bag of cooked filling into an ice bath to cool for 3 minutes.
5. Preheat oven to 350°F.
6. Roll out one sheet of puff pastry to fit a 9" x 13" pan. Place puff pastry in the pan and add cool apple filling.
7. Roll out second piece of puff pastry and place on top of the filling. Crimp the edges of the puff pastry to seal them together.
8. Cut 1 inch slits in the top, evenly across, to vent.
9. Brush with milk and sprinkle with sugar.
10. Bake for 30 minutes or until puff pastry is golden brown.
11. Allow to cool before serving!

Nutrition

Calories: 306 Sodium: 80 mg, Dietary Fiber: 4.2g, Fat: 10.5g, Carbs: 51.3g, Protein: 1.3g

Mini Lemon Cheesecakes

Tart lemons and creamy sweet cheese come together for an amazing dessert in this recipe.

Servings: 4
Prep time: 15 minutes
Cook time: 90 minutes

- 1 cup graham cracker crumbs
- 1 tablespoon unsalted butter, room temperature
- 1 (8 ounce) package neufchatel cheese
- ½ cup granulated sugar
- ¼ cup sour cream
- 2 eggs
- 1 Meyer lemon, zested
- 4 tablespoons fresh Meyer lemon juice
- 8 (4 ounce) mason jars

For raspberry sauce:

- 1 (12 ounce package) raspberries
- 1 tablespoon Meyer lemon juice
- 6 tablespoons sugar
- ¼ cup water

1. Preheat water bath to 176°F.
2. Blend graham cracker crumbs and the butter together in a mixing bowl to make cheesecake crust.
3. Spoon mixture evenly into each mason jar and press to form the crust.
4. Whip the sugar, sour cream, and cheese together in a mixing bowl, with a hand mixer, until smooth.
5. Incorporate the eggs until smooth.
6. Add batter evenly to mason jars, screw lids on tight, and place in water bath for 90 minutes.
7. Remove cheesecakes and refrigerate for at least 4 hours or overnight to set.
8. Prepare raspberry sauce by adding water to a saucepan and heat on high to boil.
9. Whisk in sugar until just smooth and fold in raspberries and lemon juice. Cover with a lid, turn to medium, and steep for 2 minutes.
10. Uncover and stir until a sauce is formed; transfer to a mason jar to cool and refrigerate until ready to serve.
11. Top each mini cheesecake with raspberry sauce to serve.

Nutrition

Calories: 539 Sodium: 474 mg, Dietary Fiber: 7.3g, Fat: 24g, Carbs: 74.4g, Protein: 11.4g

Bourbon Infusion
Apple Pie

The sweet of apple and smoky bourbon really bring something special to life in this delicious dessert drink.

Servings: 2 - 4
Prep time:
Cook time: 3 hours

2 honeycrisp apples
3 cinnamon sticks
1 vanilla bean, split lengthwise
1 teaspoon nutmeg
1 teaspoon ground allspice
1 teaspoon ginger
2 cups Kentucky bourbon, like Maker's Mark

1. Preheat a water bath to 140°F.
2. Core and chop apples into ¼ inch pieces.
3. Combine the apple pieces with the remaining ingredients in a sous vide bag or Mason jar then seal and place in the water bath.
4. Cook for 3 hours.
5. Prepare an ice bath with 1/2 ice and 1/2 water. Remove the bag or Mason jar from the water bath and place in the ice bath for 15 to 20 minutes.
6. Strain the bourbon into a large mason jar and store sealed until ready to serve over ice or warmed for a hot winter drink.

Nutrition
Calories: 319 Sodium: 3 mg, Dietary Fiber: 6g, Fat: 0.4g, Carbs: 17g, Protein: 0.6g

Sweet Meyer Lemon
Cheesecake
with Raspberry Sauce

Meyer lemons are out of this world when you use them as the start of any dessert - especially topped with sweet raspberries.

Servings: 4
Prep time: 20 minutes
Cook time: 8 hrs 90 minutes

- 1 (8 ounce) package neufchatel cheese
- ½ cup granulated sugar
- ¼ cup sour cream
- 2 eggs
- 1 lemon, zested
- 4 tablespoons fresh lemon juice
- 1 cup graham cracker crumbs
- 1 tablespoon unsalted butter, room temperature
- 8 (4 ounce) mason jars

For the topping:
Blueberries
Powdered sugar

1. Preheat water bath to 176°F.
2. Blend graham cracker crumbs and the butter together in a mixing bowl to make cheesecake crust.
3. Spoon mixture evenly into each mason jar and press to form the crust.
4. Whip the sugar, sour cream, and cheese together in a mixing bowl, with a hand mixer, until smooth.
5. Incorporate the eggs until smooth.
6. Add batter evenly to mason jars, screw lids on tight, and place in water bath for 90 minutes.
7. Remove cheesecakes and refrigerate for at least 4 hours or overnight to set.
8. Top each mini cheesecake with blueberries and powdered sugar to serve chilled.

Nutrition
Calories: 442 Sodium: 475 mg, Dietary Fiber: 2.2g, Fat: 23.6g, Carbs: 49.5g, Protein: 10.6g

Sous Vide
Lemon Curd

Scrumptious lemon curd can be used to top cakes, muffins, and even scones - but you might just want to use this recipe in your next lemon meringue pie.

Servings: 6 - 10
Prep time: 15 minutes
Cook time: 1 hour

10 egg yolks

6 lemons, zested & juiced (about 1 cup fresh lemon juice)

1 1/2 cups sugar

1 1/2 sticks butter, melted and cooled

4 (8 ounce) mason jars

1. Set your sous vide to 167°F.
2. Blend the sugar and the lemon zest, in a food processor or blender, until the sugar is a fine powder and the zest has infused into the sugar.
3. Add 1 cup of fresh lemon juice and blend.
4. Add the egg yolks, one at a time allowing each one to incorporate fully before adding the next.
5. While the food processor is running, pour the melted butter into the mixture.
6. Strain the mixture through a super fine mesh strainer to remove foam.
7. Add evenly to mason jars, seal tight.
8. Place in water bath and cook for 1 hour.
9. Remove to cool before using for your favorite dessert recipes.

Nutrition
Calories: 298 Sodium: 106 mg, Dietary Fiber: 1g, Fat: 18.4g, Carbs: 33.9g, Protein: 3.2g

Elegant Red Wine Poached Pears

Warm weather desserts are also delicious when whipped up in your sous vide container like these decadent Red Wine Poached Pears.

Servings: 4
Prep time: 15 minutes
Cook time: 1 hour

4 ripe Bosc pears, peeled
1 cup dry red wine, like Merlot or Shiraz
½ cup granulated sugar
¼ cup sweet vermouth
1 teaspoon sea salt
3 (3 inch) slices orange zest
1 vanilla bean, scraped
Vanilla bean ice cream, for serving

1. Preheat sous vide to 175°F.
2. Place all of the ingredients, except the ice cream, in a resealable plastic bag and seal.
3. Immerse in water bath and cook for 1 hour; make sure the bag remains completely submerged.
4. Remove the bag and remove pears to a cutting board.
5. Cut in half and core each pear.
6. Divide between 4 shallow bowls and top with vanilla bean ice cream.
7. Drizzle with some of the red wine liquid and serve.

Nutrition

Calories: 319 Sodium: 488 mg, Dietary Fiber: 8.5g, Fat: 2.1g, Carbs: 66.9g, Protein: 1.8g

Made in the USA
Monee, IL
16 November 2020